"I've been in student ministry since I was a student myself. After 35 years, I realized how much more there was to learn about Gen Z when it occurred to me that my two sons were part of it. Thank God for Tim McKnight! He has been more than a trusted friend to me. He's become a voice in reaching Gen Z with the gospel. He is respected by his peers and those who lead teenagers (and those who influence them) as one of the foremost leaders in preparing youth pastors to disciple a generation that seems to be so distracted by screens and social media. But what Tim does in these pages is lay out a biblical framework for helping students see who Jesus is, understand the good news of his kingdom, and become true followers of Christ. This book is a gift to the church."

—Clayton King
Founder, Crossroads Summer Camps
Teaching Pastor, Newspring Church

"I read Tim McKnight's new book *Engaging Generation Z: Raising the Bar for Youth Ministry* from cover to cover with this question in mind: 'Is there anything new under the sun to inspire kids to love God and impact their world?' He more than answered my question. The 'raised bar' Tim champions is the ancient wisdom of caring parents, rites of passage, strong, Christ-centered families, passionate youth leaders that model servanthood, a lifestyle of evangelism, and Bible-centered discipleship. The great thing about this book is that Tim demonstrates how to make that happen. Read it thoughtfully and be prepared to change your parenting and grandparenting."

—Ron Boehme
Elder, Youth With A Mission
Professor of Leadership and Intercultural Studies, Faith International University

"The vast majority of people who surrender to Jesus as Lord and Savior do it before the age of eighteen. Because of this truth, the youth ministry in every local church must be empowered and equipped to be the front lines of our evangelism and mobilization efforts. That's why *Engaging Generation Z*, by Tim McKnight, is such an important and timely book. Let this resource help guide you in reaching Gen Z, because I truly believe they are the generation in which God could spark the next great spiritual awakening! Therefore, every pastor, next gen leader, parent, and student needs this book."

—Shane Pruitt
National Next Gen Director, North American Mission Board (NAMB)
Author of *9 Common Lies Christians Believe*

"We do youth ministry best when we know our students and our Bibles well. In this book, Dr. Tim McKnight combines a rich knowledge of Scripture with a wealth of insights on the experiences and perspectives of Generation Z to deliver a blueprint for revitalized and effective youth ministry. This is an invaluabl⌷ ⌷raging resource for anyone navigating the intricac⌷ ⌷text."

—Greg Stier
⌷r, Dare 2 Share Ministries

"In his new book, *Engaging Generation Z*, Tim McKnight offers a great challenge in leading youth ministry to an ever-changing culture. Tim asks great questions to get you thinking, makes strong statements to give you a push, and offers great ideas to help advance youth ministry. Youth leaders and parents need to work through *Engaging Generation Z: Raising the Bar for Youth Ministry*, so together, we can raise the level of excellence for the students we serve."

—Randall J Davis
CEO/Executive Director, National Network of Youth Ministries

"In every era of student ministry, there is a resource that accurately assesses the landscape of the culture, identifies the unique characteristics of the current culture, and provides the practical insights necessary to faithfully serve youth and their families. In *Engaging Generation Z*, my friend Tim McKnight provides this generation's resource for ministers, leaders, and parents who are investing in today's students. His balanced approach is biblically rooted, historically informed, culturally relevant, and practically instructive. This work will be the benchmark in student ministry for years to come!"

—R. Scott Pace
Vice President for Undergraduate Studies and Dean, The College at Southeastern
Johnny Hunt Chair of Biblical Preaching

"Eager to inspire and activate your young disciples? Your search is over. In this book, author Tim McKnight coaches pastors and parents with historical perspectives from his work as a scholar and real-life narratives from his heart as a parent. Most importantly, his wisdom and encouragement come from God's Word. Prepare to see your ministry and results change as you engage Gen Z."

—Kenneth S. Coley
Senior Professor of Christian Education
Southeastern Baptist Theological Seminary

ENGAGING
GENERATION
Z

Raising the Bar
for Youth Ministry

TIM McKNIGHT

KREGEL
MINISTRY

Engaging Generation Z: Raising the Bar for Youth Ministry

© 2021 by Tim McKnight

Published by Kregel Ministry, an imprint of Kregel Publications, 2450 Oak Industrial Dr. NE, Grand Rapids, MI 49505-6020.

ISBN 978-0-8254-4593-4

Printed in the United States of America

22 23 24 25 26 / 6 5 4 3

To my mom, Mary Ann McKnight.
You showed me more than anyone what it
looks like to raise the bar in youth ministry.
Thank you for the example you gave me in
your over twenty years in youth ministry.
I love you.

CONTENTS

Foreword by Greg Stier...9

Acknowledgments 11

Introduction: Every Generation Must Be Taught Anew...........13

PART 1: TEST TIME: DOES YOUTH MINISTRY PASS?

1. The World Has Changed, but the Gospel Has Not:
   Analyzing the Current Culture of Student Ministry 19

2. Meet Generation Z: The Next Great Generation 31

3. The Potency of Expectancy: Why We Can Be Optimistic...........47

4. Truth or Consequences: Biblical Teaching Confronts
   Contemporary Practice..57

5. Entertaining Children or Assembling an Army?:
   Lessons from History 65

6. From the Parachurch to the Local Church:
   A Brief History of Youth Ministry 77

PART 2: REINVENTING YOUTH MINISTRY

7. Teaching the Youth Well: Building a Ministry on the Word........93

8. Habitual Love: Stirring the Affections of Youth 109

9. Get Real: Sharing Jesus Consistently 123

10. Life Is Worship: Recalibrating the Focus of Students 135

11. Advice to Parents: It's Time to Grow Up................................151

12. Meanwhile, Back at the Church: Staff Relations
    and Leading a Ministry 171

13. Rites of Passage: Seasons of Change......................................183

Conclusion: Raise the Bar 195

FOREWORD

I've always been a big Bruce Lee fan. His lighting-fast kicks, one-inch punches and amazing nunchuck skills left me in awe when I first saw his Hollywood-produced movie *Enter the Dragon*.

The first thing I did after seeing the movie was to go out and buy myself some nunchucks. I wanted to swing those two chain-connected pieces of wood so fast that they would sound like a small army of angry hummingbirds to all the imaginary opponents I would soon be "fighting" in my room.

The problem is that I was never trained by someone who actually knew what they were doing. Over the course of countless months, I endured several self-inflicted injuries. From hitting myself in the back of the head to clunking the inside of my elbow bone to the much-dreaded nunchuck-to-the-groin, I spent half of my time on the floor of my room groaning, moaning, and trying to recover.

But I persisted in spite of the bumps and bruises. Over the course of a few years of trial, error, and injuries, I got relatively good. Though not at the Bruce Lee level of nunchuck excellence, I can make those two pieces of wood, now hanging in my office, hum.

In many ways, learning nunchucks is like learning youth ministry. It goes much better if you have a skilled sensei training you than just trying to wing it and learn it on your own. Someone who knows both God's Word (2 Tim. 3:16–17) and "understands the times" we are living in (1 Chr. 12:32) will take you to the next level of youth ministry without nearly as many bumps, bruises, and self-induced knockouts.

That's why I'm thrilled that you have chosen to read *Engaging Generation Z: Raising the Bar for Youth Ministry* by my friend Dr. Tim McKnight. In this book he will teach you the basics of what it's going to take to reach, disciple, and mobilize the next generation for gospel advancers.

His mastery of God's Word will ground you in a biblical approach to youth ministry. Every chapter is soaked in Scripture (the ultimate youth ministry manual) and built on the timeless foundation of God's Word.

Tim does an excellent job of stretching your thinking when it comes to building a gospel-advancing ministry that both reaches the lost and disciples the believers. He calls moms and dads to be the primary youth leaders without forsaking the necessary reality of youth ministry in a fatherless and broken-home culture.

But the other side of the nunchuck is equally balanced. He "understands the times" and unpacks the challenges, temptations, mindsets, and strongholds that Gen Z is facing. You will finish this book knowing the extreme challenges teenagers face today and the amazing opportunities they have to reach their world and this world with the hope of Christ like never before.

To top it all off, Dr. Tim McKnight not only teaches youth ministry; he holds a second degree black belt in karate. His Instagram name is @peacefulwarriorllc. And he teaches Kenpo Jiu Jitsu on the side!

Although these facts may not help you do youth ministry any better, they may help you pay a little closer attention to his book just in case he asks you about it!

By reading this book, you are allowing Tim to be your sensei in youth ministry. When you're finished with it, you may not be able to wield nunchucks like Bruce Lee, but you'll be able to do youth ministry a lot more like Jesus.

—Greg Stier

ACKNOWLEDGMENTS

Numerous people deserve my thanks for their assistance in writing this second edition of *Raising the Bar*. I first want to thank the author of the first edition, Alvin Reid, who had the vision and foresight to raise the bar in youth ministry and say things that youth ministry educators and youth pastors were just beginning to discover to be true. His fingerprints and content from the first edition are still evident in this second edition. I appreciate the opportunity and trust he extended to me in inviting me to write this second edition of the book.

My colleagues in youth ministry also contributed in numerous ways to this volume. I've benefited from conversations with youth ministry veterans like Ken Coley and Richard Ross. They've spoken with wisdom and insight in numerous conferences gatherings of professors and leaders in youth ministry that I've attended. Clayton King is a consistent friend and encouragement in the ministry. He invited me to be one of the speakers for Clayton King Ministries. In that capacity, I interacted with a number of youth pastors and students across the country. These interactions helped fuel the chapters that follow and gave me great encouragement for what the Lord is doing in youth ministries across the country that are raising the bar. Greg Stier is a catalyst for evangelism in youth ministry, whose belief in the potential for students to reach their peers with the gospel and to spark a national revival is both inspiring and contagious. I appreciate his friendship and willingness to write the foreword for the book.

The administration, faculty, staff, and students of Anderson University's College of Christian Studies and Clamp Divinity School are a consistent blessing in my life. I thank my boss and dean, Dr. Michael Duduit, for his encouragement during this project and for his willingness to allow me to carry a lighter semester during its final stages. My colleagues in the college and divinity school are an inspiration to me as shepherds of their classrooms and scholars of the highest order. They encourage me to stay sharp and to pursue excellence in the classroom. The students I have the privilege to teach are such a blessing, especially my youth ministry students. They serve faithfully in church youth ministries while carrying heavy class loads. They display a genuine love for the teenagers, parents, and adult leaders they serve. It's such a privilege to walk with them during this stage of their journey in ministry.

My youth pastor from my first years in a youth group, John Riley, showed me what the love of Christ looked like. He was the person God used to start drawing me to Christ. I'm eternally grateful for the love that John consistently showed us as our youth pastor. He raised the bar for me regarding what it looks like to be a great youth pastor.

I'm thankful for my mom and dad. Thanks, Dad, for showing me that a Christian man can be humble and love Christ while at the same time being a noble warrior. Thanks to Mom for always caring and seeking to show God's plan for me and how he could use me in ministry. It was such a privilege to have my mom as my youth minister my senior year of high school.

Thanks to my in-laws Richard and Connie Heintzelman for raising such a great woman of God who would become my wife. I appreciate your consistent love and encouragement for whatever wild-haired project your son-in-law tackles. You are both a blessing!

To my children: Noah, thanks for your encouraging words. Micah, thank you for your tender heart. Karissa, thank you for those rides back from preaching events singing '80s music together. MaryAnna, thank you for the joyful spirit you always bring.

Angela, you are my greatest earthy treasure, my soul mate, and my partner in ministry. Thank you for saying, "Yes."

To my Lord and Savior Jesus Christ, I am nothing without You. Thank You for saving me through your infinite grace and mercy!

INTRODUCTION

EVERY GENERATION MUST BE TAUGHT ANEW

Give ear, O my people, to my teaching;
incline your ears to the words of my mouth!
I will open my mouth in a parable;
I will utter dark sayings from of old,
things that we have heard and known,
that our fathers have told us.
We will not hide them from their children,
but tell to the coming generation
the glorious deeds of the LORD, and his might,
and the wonders that he has done.
He established a testimony in Jacob
and appointed a law in Israel,
which he commanded our fathers
to teach to their children,
that the next generation might know them,
the children yet unborn,
and arise and tell them to their children,
so that they should set their hope in God
and not forget the works of God,
but keep his commandments;
and that they should not be like their fathers,
a stubborn and rebellious generation,
a generation whose heart was not steadfast,
whose spirit was not faithful to God.
                                        —Psalm 78:1–8

In this psalm, Asaph expresses his concern that the people of Israel
pass down their faith in God and knowledge of his redemptive acts

in their history to the next generation. He mentions that parents, particularly fathers, must teach their children the Word of God so that the next generation will trust in God and keep his commands. Asaph hopes that such instruction and modeling by parents and members of the faith community will grant the next generation a firm foundation and help it avoid the sins and rebellion of previous generations.

It is easy to resonate with Asaph's concern. We want our children to know the redemptive work of God and to have their lives transformed by the gospel. We pray they walk in obedience to God with hearts motivated by love for him. We hope they will discern false teaching, opinions, and behaviors that are destructive and contrary to Scripture and God's will for their lives. We understand that the years of childhood and adolescence are critical for their spiritual development.

The teen years, or the years primarily targeted by youth ministry, are in many ways the most important years of a person's life. More seeds of ministry are sown in youth between the ages of twelve and eighteen, more relationships forged that affect their future, more choices made with long-term implications, than arguably any other period in life. According to one Barna survey, 76 percent of Christians accept Christ before the age of twenty-one.[1] Young adults are beginning to think about issues that will influence the rest of their lives. These are the days when they develop their own worldview and their own faith and spirituality.

Are we doing a good job preparing them? This book doesn't indict contemporary youth ministry. Rather, part 1 discusses how the evangelical church is doing in preparing youth, students, or young adults (I will use the three terms synonymously) to face the adult world. And more than that, how are we doing in preparing them to cross that line in the sand? This book does not present a surefire formula for creating the ideal youth ministry of the twenty-first century. Rather, part 2 suggests areas in which the potential of youth may be unleashed.

---

1   George Barna, "Survey: Christians Are Not Spreading the Gospel," GeorgeBarna.com, November 30, 2017, http://www.georgebarna.com/research-flow/2017/11/30/survey-christians-are-not-spreading-the-gospel.

Youth are not finishing childhood; they are young adults preparing for adulthood. They will rise to the bar we set for them. We can give them encouragement through a word of praise, a pat on the back, or a hug. But sometimes the best encouragement is a kick in the pants.

Sometimes, however, it is we, the leaders, who need the kick in the pants. Whether you're a pastor, youth pastor, youth worker, parent, or any combination thereof, may the words that follow challenge you to get out of your comfort zone in working with and discipling youth, encourage you about the quality of young people today, and help you reevaluate how you see the youth in your life.

This new generation is poised to make a difference—to *change* the world to the glory of God. May we serve as Christ followers who raise the bar for the students following us.

And let's start *today.*

PART 1

TEST TIME:
DOES YOUTH MINISTRY PASS?

Imagine Jesus taking his disciples up to a mountain. He gathers them around and teaches them for a while, saying, "Blessed are the poor in spirit, for theirs is the kingdom of heaven. Blessed are they that mourn. Blessed are the meek. Blessed are the merciful. Blessed are they that search for justice."

> Then Simon Peter asks, "Do we have to write this down?"
> And Andrew asks, "Will this be on the test?"
> And Philip says, "I don't have a pencil."
> And James asks, "Do we have to turn this in?"
> And John says, "That's not fair. The other disciples didn't have to learn this."
> And Judas asks, "What does this have to do with real life?"

Then one of the religious authorities standing nearby asks, "Where is your lesson plan and the teaching outline of your major points? Where is your anticipatory set and learning objectives in the cognitive domain?"

And Jesus wept.

In a perfect world, students would never have to take exams or quizzes. Professors would never have to grade tests or papers.

Because students would be so motivated to learn that they would devour their assignments and miss class only for an appendectomy or a concussion.

But this is not a perfect world. We need to conduct tests to ensure that students are ready to meet the challenges of adult life. Suppose, for example, that a member of your church has a brain tumor. The young surgeon tells you prior to the surgery, "I've read the books, watched some operations, and have complete confidence in my ability . . . but no one's ever tested me to see if I can, in fact, successfully perform the surgery." Would you want that young surgeon to operate on your sick member?

Suppose, now, that your dear uncle Joe is unsaved and that you've been praying for him for twenty years. A young person says to you, "I've attended youth meetings since grade school, and I've participated in the usual church activities for youth." Would you want that young person to witness to your uncle Joe?

Ministry deals with eternity—a matter more vital than even brain surgery. You may or may not agree with much of what this book has to say about youth ministry, but consider this: outside the church students are tested both academically and physically. Does it not make sense for youth in our churches to take spiritual tests to prepare for entering fallen world as capable adults?

Youth in church are underchallenged and treated like children. We need to raise the bar to produce biblical champions.

If we gave spiritual tests to the students in our churches, tests with a standard comparable to a physical fitness test or an academic exam such as the SAT, the vast majority would probably fail miserably. And the fault would not lie with them. Many parents complain about low academic standards in some of our public schools. But has the church considered what kind of standard we are setting in preparing a generation of young adults?

I issue a challenge. We can raise the bar for this generation. But we can't do it unless we admit that the bar has been set too low for too long.

1

THE WORLD HAS CHANGED, BUT THE GOSPEL HAS NOT
ANALYZING THE CURRENT CULTURE OF STUDENT MINISTRY

> Besides this you know the time, that the hour has
> come for you to wake from sleep. For salvation
> is nearer to us now than when we first believed.
> The night is far gone; the day is at hand. So then
> let us cast off the works of darkness and put on
> the armor of light. Let us walk properly as in
> the daytime, not in orgies and drunkenness,
> not in sexual immorality and sensuality, not in
> quarreling and jealousy.
> —Romans 13:11–13

In February 2003, the unthinkable happened. Jesica Santillan was wheeled into an operating room at one of the most prestigious hospitals in the world. She'd been sick from infancy, but Jesica and her family believed that the complicated operation, involving a rare heart-lung transplant, would give her weakened body new life.

The transplant seemed to go well. Then the horrible mistake was discovered. The transplanted heart and lungs were of the wrong blood type. Days later, following a second attempt at a transplant, Jesica died. Having the right hospital, right doctors, right procedure, but a wrong match spelled disaster.

Something has gone wrong, too, in the hospitals and operating rooms for the soul. Across America today, many gifted, committed youth ministers and workers, as well as pastors and parents, long to see youth thrive. This current generation of youth has the potential for revival, for renewal, for change. But the church faces a problem—the youth-ministry approaches we have been using are the wrong match. They have failed to develop the potential of youth. We cannot say that, over the past two decades or so, we have raised up a generation of students who have changed the world for Christ.

Over the past few years, I've met with student-ministry leaders on the local, state, and national levels. In every one of those meetings we discussed the trend of students leaving church youth groups across the nation. In the book *You Lost Me*, David Kinnaman laments, "The ages eighteen to twenty-nine are a black hole of church attendance; this age segment is 'missing in action' from most congregations."[1] Kinnaman was writing about trends among Millennials, yet the statistics regarding Generation Z students are equally disturbing. Ben Trueblood, director of student ministry for Lifeway Christian Resources, notes, "We found that 66 percent of students who were active in their church during high school no longer remained active in the church between ages 18–22."[2] Though we rightly have shifted away from event-driven youth ministries to focus more on family-equipping youth-ministry strategies, more than half of the students in our youth groups still leave the church. The numbers become more staggering when we consider how effective we have been at reaching unchurched students.

About a decade after youth ministry improved by focusing more on parents and the family, the situation has not changed a great deal. We have failed to produce a generation of young people who leave youth groups ready to change the world for Christ. Rather, 66 percent of them leave the church after graduation.

Now, before you decide that we need to shift away from a focus on families and parents, let me say quickly that I don't think a family-equipping approach to youth ministry is responsible for the continued exodus of high school graduates from churches. Yet the failure of contemporary youth ministry to make a positive impact on

---

1 David Kinnaman, *You Lost Me* (Grand Rapids: Baker, 2011), 22.
2 Ben Trueblood, *Within Reach* (Nashville: Lifeway, 2018), 12.

youth culture cannot be ignored. *If we keep doing what we're doing, we'll keep getting what we're getting!*

This book will not list everything wrong with contemporary youth ministry or present a quick fix for the problem. But my research and experience reveal a common denominator: churches across America treat teenagers like fourth-graders rather than disciples. As youth ministers and parents, we need to set a new example and a new standard. We can grow disciples who advance the gospel and the kingdom of Christ while they are students and after they graduate. We can mobilize students who have a kingdom mindset and pursue a kingdom mission.

The Power of God

Have you ever lived in a town where half the residents became radical, fanatical followers of Jesus in a couple of years? Have you lived in a neighborhood where instead of sports, clothes, or cars, the subject of conversation for almost everyone was Jesus?

That was the kind of world in which Jonathan Edwards found himself about 250 years ago. In the eighteenth century, God shook the American colonies in a revival movement known as the First Great Awakening. Edwards wrote the treatise *Some Thoughts Concerning the Present Revival of Religion in New England* to describe and defend the movement. This young pastor noticed something most ministers have failed to recognize since: when God begins a new movement of his Spirit, he often uses young people at the heart of it. Note Edwards's comment about the great revival he observed:

> The work has been chiefly amongst the young; and comparatively but few others have been made partakers of it. And indeed it has commonly been so, when God has begun any great work for the revival of his church; he has taken the young people, and has cast off the old and stiff-necked generation.[3]

---

3 Jonathan Edwards, "Some Thoughts Concerning the Present Revival of Religion in New England, and the Way in Which It Ought to Be Acknowledged

While the present-day potential for revival is promising, let's face it—student ministry can be just plain hard. Youth leaders today have incredible love for young people and a passion to see them grow in Christ, but they often report being worn out from ministry. Greg Stier summarizes what I hear often from youth pastors:

> Maybe it's the complaints about the stains in the carpets or the holes in the walls in the youth room. Perhaps it's the struggle of the juggle—the constant juggling act between parental and pastoral expectations. As a result of those difficulties and a thousand others, many youth leaders eventually give in or give up. They give in to the counter-biblical challenge to reel in their students' exuberance instead of harnessing it and focusing it. They give up on going for the optimum, on stirring the pot, and on swinging for the fences. . . . The result is that youth leaders often slowly transform their roles from passionate visionary to skilled event-coordinator, from mission-driven general to sanctified baby-sitter.[4]

Many youth ministers are simply sick and tired of being sick and tired. But as a professor who enjoys critical analysis, playing the devil's advocate, and the opportunity to evaluate movements or theories, I'm increasingly unimpressed with some of the attitudes and approaches used in youth ministry today.

Don't get me wrong—I see good in many youth ministries, and I love youth pastors. I teach some of the finest people studying for youth ministry on the planet. But one thing is clear: most youth pastors learn youth ministry from youth pastors who learned youth ministry from youth pastors. Such inbreeding does not encourage serious reflection

---

and Promoted, Humbly Offered to the Public, in a Treatise on That Subject," in *The Works of Jonathan Edwards*, 2 vols., ed. Sereno E. Dwight (1834; repr., London: Banner of Truth Trust, n.d.), 1:423.

4   Greg Stier, *Outbreak: Creating a Contagious Youth Ministry through Viral Evangelism* (Chicago: Moody, 2002), 17.

on ministry practices. Add to that the rapid growth of youth ministry as a separate discipline in the modern church, and it is little wonder that neither the opportunity nor the time has been afforded for the church or for youth ministers to analyze this field critically.

It is time to assess the state of youth ministry. An honest, straightforward critique of basic presuppositions and attitudes is needed, as well as an evaluation of the impact that the many cottage industries, various parachurch organizations, and youth ministries in churches across America are making in the real world where youth live.

In a nutshell, we must evaluate how the church relates the truth of Christianity to culture. In Romans 13:11, Paul challenges us to be aware of our culture. His saying, "And now, *knowing the time*," does not mean we should be looking at our watches. The Greek term he uses refers to an intimate, personal knowledge of the season, or the climate, in which we live. In other words, just as preachers of the Word must be able to exegete Scripture, so too must leaders in the church be able to analyze culture.

Contemporary popular culture treats youth as children, not young adults. Popular culture—from YouTube to movies to video games—thrives on maintaining a distinct youth culture for marketing purposes. In the church, attitudes are not much better. Christian publications and church or parachurch youth ministries deal with the particular, most pressing needs of the times—how to say no to sex, dealing with peer pressure, and so on. They address behavior rather than the heart, furthering the trend of moralistic therapeutic deism seen in many churches and church student ministries.[5]

All of these and many more issues are vital, but none of them addresses our basic philosophical approach to young people. Do we

---

5   Christian Smith and Melinda Denton state, "Moralistic Therapeutic Deism is about inculcating a moralistic approach to life. It teaches that central to living a good and happy life is being a good moral person. That means being nice, kind, pleasant, respectful, responsible, at work on self-improvement, taking care of one's health, and doing one's best to be successful." Christian Smith and Melinda Lundquist Denton, *Soul Searching: The Religious and Spiritual Lives of American Teenagers* (Oxford: Oxford University Press, 2009), 163.

see young people as children finishing childhood and thus in need of activities to keep them occupied, or do we see them as young adults who are disciples ready to engage the challenges of a complex world?

God has assembled an army of young adults. He has opened a door before the leaders of the church today through which to see a generation of radicals ready to be unleashed on the culture. Yet today, they are the most overlooked army in the church. Consider this: youth are

- utilized by cultists (look at the thousands of young people who take an annual Mormon mission, for example), but ignored by the church;
- enlisted by our government in times of war, but too often left on the sidelines of spiritual conflict;
- chosen to represent nations at the highest level of athletic endeavor, but pushed aside into secondary status in the body of the Christ;
- often challenged academically in school, but fed spiritual baby food in church;
- poised to live for Christ, but too often told to stay out of the way.

Why should you focus on youth ministry? *First,* as already noted, over the years there has been an exodus of youth out of the church.

Second, a historical study of spiritual awakenings has raised the question, "Why hasn't more been written on the role of youth in the activity of God?" (Perhaps because adults write church history texts?)

Third, discussions with colleagues and others led to the conclusion that current youth ministry has not been effective. The cottage industries related to youth ministry are, although financially lucrative, spiritually anemic. Thousands of students attend various inspirational events, but those events have not been effective in taking students from an adolescent mindset to focusing on doing great things for God and to advance the kingdom of Christ. Youth ministers—including many in my classes as well as scores with whom I have talked over the past few years—indicate a growing dissatisfaction with the present state of youth ministry. Who can blame them, with a church culture that treats teens like fourth-graders and youth pastors like babysitters?

Fourth, if all politics is local, then everything spiritual is personal. I have four teenagers at home: Noah and Micah (both 18), Karissa (16), and MaryAnna (11). I can write and preach and teach and make all sorts of bold declarations, but I have only one chance to raise my children. Across America, millions of Christian parents feel the same way. Focusing on youth ministry, then, not only analyzes a subject but also represents the effort of a fellow pilgrim trying to find God's best for his children and the children of others.

Evaluation Is a Healthy Thing

Louie Giglio has been a strategic leader in a movement called Passion that has helped many students rethink worship. His thoughts on youth ministry offer a succinct overview of what I have also observed:

> First, we need innovative leaders, those who blaze a trail with fresh creativity and *not just a rehashed imitation of the current culture.* Second, *we must have a belief in our students' capacity to grasp more.* . . . Third, we as leaders must . . . *"show the way" and not just "tell the way."* And fourth, we must have a clear strategy so that at the end of the day we don't just have a pile of extended energy but rather the assurance that we've accomplished the goal.[6]

The meteoric growth of youth ministry in the church over the past generation calls for analysis, evaluation, and reflection. Why? Note the following excerpt from an article by Mark DeVries:

> Although her family was only nominally involved in the church, Jenny came to our youth group faithfully throughout

---

6 Louie Giglio, foreword to Andy Stanley and Stuart Hall, *The Seven Checkpoints* (West Monroe, LA: Howard, 2001), x, emphasis added.

her teenage years. She went on mission trips and attended Sunday school; she was a regular fixture in our program. We had been successful with Jenny, or so we thought.

Jimmy, on the other hand, never quite connected with our youth ministry. We really worked to get him involved with our youth programs. He had no interest in retreats or mission trips; Sunday school bored him, and youth groups seemed a little on the silly side for his taste. He sometimes attended another church across town. On my little scoreboard of kids we had been effective with, Jimmy was on the "lost" side.

But Jimmy had one thing going for him—every Sunday, he was in worship—with his parents at our church or with his friends at another church. Jimmy didn't need our outrageous and creative youth ministry to lead him to faith maturity.

But for Jenny, our youth ministry was her only Christian connection. Unlike a real family, the youth group "family" forced her to resign when she was too old to fit the requirements. She now looks back on her youth group experience as . . . a fun, even laughable part of her past, but something that belongs exclusively in the realm of her teenage years.

There is something wrong with the standard of success that prematurely rates a leader's work with Jenny as the example of success and Jimmy's as the example of failure.[7]

More than a few youth pastors say that the above story is not a rare one. The following e-mail has become familiar:

After 11 years of youth ministry I say that [DeVries's story] is not an exceptional example. I sit with tears in my eyes

---

7   Mark DeVries, "What Is Youth Ministry's Relationship to the Family?," in *Reaching a Generation for Christ,* eds. Richard R. Dunn and Mark H. Centers III (Chicago: Moody, 1997), 484–85.

as I think of all my Jennys. Their names are different . . .
but it hurts all the same. DeVries is so on the money when
he says we must tie [our youth] to the family—first, their
nuclear family, and then the family of God—in a much
more meaningful way. If we don't, they simply outgrow
their faith. I am working to change the trend and raise the
bar here! —Cliff

The Barna Group reports, "The percentage of people whose
beliefs qualify them for a biblical worldview declines in each suc-
cessively younger generation: 10 percent of Boomers, 7 percent
of Gen X, and 6 percent of Millennials have a biblical worldview,
compared to only 4 percent of Gen Z."[8] This same study of students
further concludes, "Many in Generation Z, more than in generations
before them, are a spiritual blank slate. They are drawn to things
spiritual, but their starting point is vastly different from previous
generations, many of whom received a basic education on the Bible
and Christianity."[9]

While these statistics and trends pose a challenge, I see an opportunity for parents and people serving in student ministry. Having lived
in Okinawa and on the Gulf Coast, I've encountered a number of
typhoons and hurricanes. These storms do not develop independently.
Several natural forces converge at just the right time—or, if you're in
the path of the storm, the wrong time.

As in the development of a hurricane/typhoon, several forces seem
to be converging on the church. *First,* over the past several years I've
met youth pastors all over the nation who feel much the same—they
love youth ministry and youth, but they are frustrated with the current
state of youth ministry. Many recognize the need for a reformation of
youth ministry, yet most I meet have more questions than answers.

The *second* force is the new generation, Generation Z, the largest
generation in the history of our nation.

---

8 Barna Group, *Gen Z* (Barna Group and Impact 360 Institute, 2018), 25.
9 Barna Group, *Gen Z*, 26.

The *third* force arises from my generation. A growing, foaming, tsunami of parental passion has expressed itself in an explosion of everything from Christian and home schools, to parenting seminars, to the shift to family-engaged student ministry. Parents of youth and preteens want to get it right with their kids.

The *fourth* and *final* force comes from what we know about God. The forces above are not lost on our great God. He is never caught by surprise and is well aware of coming trends. In the past, God has used generations of young people in times of great revival. Might he be preparing a new generation to use in similar fashion?

One thing is certain. God *is* at work. Will we, like Barnabas in Acts 11, seek to see the hand of God in a new generation? By perpetuating the status quo, by ignoring the evidence, by failing to seek him for wisdom, or by failing to model biblical discipleship, do we honor God and help a generation?

Teenagers have power today. Barna gives examples:

- Teenagers largely define the values and leisure endeavors of our nation.
- The family is the foundation of the universe, and much in society is impacted on how youth prioritize the family.
- Finally, the future of the church will be determined by this generation's faith and commitments.[10]

Current research regarding church attendance among young people is a mixed bag. The Barna Group reports that "while a majority of teens still self identifies as 'Christian' (58 percent), only 43 percent have recently attended church, and just one in 11 is an 'engaged Christian,' with beliefs and practices that put faith front-and-center in their lives."[11] The bad news is that the shift from event-driven youth ministry to family-engaged youth ministry over the last generation has failed to produce spiritual giants.

---

10   George Barna, *Real Teens: A Contemporary Snapshot of Youth Culture* (Ventura, CA: Regal, 2001), 113.
11   Barna, *Gen Z*, 26.

These trends and statistics clearly indicate that "business as usual"—sometimes busyness as usual—in youth ministry is not making the desired impact. A pragmatic approach that ignores a biblically based, gospel-centered, family-engaged, kingdom-focused student ministry strategy will not be a "quick fix" to solve these issues. Parents and student-ministry leaders must do the heavy lifting theologically necessary to build a foundation upon which we can found effective youth ministries. We must set the example in evangelism and discipleship that our students can follow. For students to raise the bar, we first must raise our expectations of what healthy kingdom-focused, biblically based, missionally mobilized students look like. Then we must model what we want them to replicate.

A Personal Journey into Youth Ministry

Years ago psychologist Abraham Maslow developed what he called a hierarchy of needs. Everyone—no matter what background, nationality, or economic situation—has certain needs, such as food, shelter, and a sense of safety. Maslow was right but didn't go far enough. Everyone has another need also—to know God and to make a difference with her or his God-given life. Mathematician Blaise Pascal describes that need as a God-sized vacuum, or a God-shaped hole. Only Jesus can fill that hole. He does more, however, than fill it. He gives each person who receives him a passion to live out God's purpose.

Students across the country are searching for purpose and meaning in life. Parents and student-ministry leaders have the privilege of helping young people find God's purpose for their lives. We can help them live out the Great Commandment and the Great Commission in middle school and high school. They are looking to us as models for what it means to be a disciple. We can show them how to walk with Christ and lead others to do the same. God can use parents and leaders in student ministry to raise up mature disciples of Christ who demonstrate the gospel of Jesus through their words and lives while they are in middle school and high school. We can help them see what it looks like to walk with Christ and actively engage in his church after they graduate.

In Deuteronomy 30, Moses addressed the nation of Israel at a critical time. Nearing the day of crossing into the Promised Land, the new postwilderness generation needed firm spiritual footing on which to tread. Moses challenged the people with these words: "I have set before you life and death, blessing and curse. Therefore choose life" (v. 19).

The people of God stood at a crossroads, and so do we. We stand at the brink of the post-Christian world. We are not leaving the wilderness; we are entering it—a world of uncharted territory that promotes same-sex marriage, relativism, pluralism, a self-focused lifestyle, identity confusion, and tolerance (as long as we do not teach or preach that Christ is the only way to God). As you stand before a new generation, challenge them to choose life—the life found in Jesus. Challenge them to follow his way and embrace his truth. Challenge them to spend their lives in advancing the gospel and the kingdom of Christ around the world. Parents and student-ministry leaders, it's time to raise the bar!

2

MEET GENERATION Z
THE NEXT GREAT GENERATION

When Joshua dismissed the people, the people of Israel went each to his inheritance to take possession of the land. And the people served the LORD all the days of Joshua, and all the days of the elders who outlived Joshua, who had seen all the great work that the LORD had done for Israel. And Joshua the son of Nun, the servant of the LORD, died at the age of 110 years. And they buried him within the boundaries of his inheritance in Timnath-heres, in the hill country of Ephraim, north of the mountain of Gaash. And all that generation also were gathered to their fathers. And there arose another generation after them who did not know the LORD or the work that he had done for Israel.

—Judges 2:6–10

Seismic shifts have occurred in our culture over the past fifteen years. Back then, we carried flip phones that we thought were innovative. Now, we have smart phones, iPads, and mobile devices that do the work our desktop computers did years ago. We thought it was cool that we could do a video chat on our desktop or laptop computers. Now, we can speak face-to-face with someone on our phones. Technology continues to shrink the world, enabling us to interact with people or information from around the world instantaneously. These technological advances influence how and how much we interact with each other. As we will see in this chapter, they have had a tremendous impact upon Generation Z.

Another major change that occurred over the last fifteen years is the decline of Christianity in the United States. For the first time in the history of the nation, less than half of the country's population is Protestant—48 percent in 2012.[1] And the number of people with no religious affiliation continues to increase in our nation. Among members of Generation Z, only four percent hold to a biblical worldview.[2] Generation Z is the first post-Christian generation in the history of our country. They are largely a generation who does not know the Lord.

Why is it important to study generations? We need to know the culture of each generation so that we can better contextualize the gospel for its members. If we are going to raise the bar in youth ministry, we must first study the culture of the students with whom we're doing ministry.

A Critical Crossroads

Just as in the time of the book of Judges, we are witnessing a generation who does not know the Lord or his work through Jesus Christ. Judges reveals a cycle: the people of Israel rebel against the Lord, God raises up a judge to lead or deliver them, the people of Israel are convicted, they return to the worship of the Lord, and the cycle repeats.

Some scholars believe this is the cycle we see in revival and awakenings. People who claim the name of Jesus Christ stray from worshiping him and making him known through sharing the gospel and making disciples. Then God raises up preachers and missionaries who faithfully preach and live the gospel in front of backslidden church members. The preaching of the gospel convicts folks who are

---

1   Cathy Lynn Grossman, "As Protestants Decline, Those with No Religion Gain," *USA Today*, October 8, 2012, http://www.usatoday.com/story/news/nation/2012/10/08/nones-protestant-religion-pew/1618445.

2   Barna Group, *Gen Z* (Ventura: Barna Group and Impact 360 Institute, 2018), 25.

in the church, and they repent of their sins and begin to share the gospel through their lips and their lives once again. The witness of this revived group of church members impacts their family members, friends, and acquaintances. These people in the Christ followers' relational circles come to Christ, and an awakening begins to break out across communities causing both spiritual and societal change.

Our nation needs such revival and awakening. Our communities need such spiritual and societal change. If such an awakening is to occur, Christ followers in the church must first proclaim the gospel to members of the surrounding culture. Youth are a subculture within the national culture. We must know youth culture, particularly the culture of Generation Z, in order to build cultural bridges over which the gospel can travel and to break down cultural barriers that would hinder the gospel from being heard. For this reason, it is imperative that we know the culture of Generation Z.

Failure to engage Generation Z with the gospel would leave the members of this post-Christian generation without saving knowledge of Jesus Christ. Failure is not an option for parents and youth leaders. We cannot let this generation continue without the knowledge of the Lord Jesus and what he has done for us.

So, who is Generation Z?

Today's New Generation

I am the proud father of four children who are members of Generation Z. I teach as a professor at a Christian liberal arts university and speak to teens in churches, at camps, and in conferences, providing me ample opportunity to observe and interact with today's youth. Below are a few of my observations about the cultural environment of Generation Z:

1. They have no recollection of a time when our country was not at war.
2. They have instantaneous access to almost any information they want.
3. They consider '80s music "oldies music."

4. They do not understand why anyone would want to hang out at the mall.
5. They cannot fathom a time where immediate access through face-to-face video interaction or texting was not possible.
6. They will never have to listen through a cassette tape to get to the song they want to hear.
7. They have never known a time when same-sex marriage was not an option.
8. The First Gulf War is ancient history to them.
9. They think that Vans and Chuck Taylors are a new trend.
10. They have never heard the words "awesome," "gnarly," or "tubular."

Their Cultural Center

The above list offers a cultural orientation of today's students, but the events that influence this new generation are also important. The members of Generation Z witnessed two major economic recessions. They have watched helmet-camera footage on YouTube of firefights occurring in Iraq, Afghanistan, and Syria, battlefields of the now eighteen-year global War on Terror. They have not known economic or global security in their lifetime.

Yet these explosive events, although worthy of significant attention, can cause us to the miss less noticeable yet more critical long-term trends that impact American youth. By focusing on the traumatic and immediate events that capture the headlines, might we miss the larger, deeper shifts in the cultural center?

One of these shifts in the cultural center relates to generation. Some observers place too much emphasis on generational differences, but we're wise to note the climate, or the season, in which we live. And there *are* definite differences in the cultural center of each generation.

While no clear mark delineates a generational era, recent generations are typically arranged accordingly:

- Builders: Born 1927–1945
- Boomers: Born 1946–1964

- Busters: Born 1965–1981
- Millennials: Born 1982–1998
- Generation Z: Born 1999–2015

The Boomer culture was marked by borderline self-worship and could be described in the phrase "get ahead." The Buster culture could be described by the phrase "get lost." The Millennial culture could be described by the phrase "get real." The Generation Z culture could be described by the phrase "get wired."

Defining generations, though, is far from an exact science. I issue two cautions. First, every person of any culture and any generation has many things in common with other humans. Physically, spiritually, and emotionally, the similarities across the centuries are striking. All are created in the image of God, all have sinned, all need a Savior whose name is Jesus, all have the ultimate destiny of heaven or hell. So in the macroscopic view of things, generational differences—although they do matter—can easily be overemphasized.

Second, this post-Christian world—in which Generation Z will be the first full-fledged members—bears a similarity, philosophically, to that which the New Testament church faced. The pluralism and relativism of the first century have again become significant forces in culture. In such a climate, the early believers' exclusive claim that Jesus was the only way of salvation was met with hostility, even as in our day so-called "tolerance" leads many to attack evangelical believers for the gospel we share. The times they are a-changing! In determining how best to deal with this generation, we who work and live with the members of Generation Z would do well, then, to immerse ourselves in the Word.

Their Cultural Shift

That being said, obvious differences exist between generations. And to better understand how critical this generation is to a fallen world, we must compare it to earlier ones in American history.

Barna gives a good summary of the shift from Builders to Baby Boomers:

If there was ever a group that should have understood the need to enter the cultural scene with a major statement, it should have been the Boomers. After all, they had replaced the Builder generation in the '60s with a series of high-profile, in-your-face transitions. Elvis Presley and Chuck Berry, the most radical musical pioneers adored by the last of the Builder teens, were positively angelic in comparison to the wild hair, daring lyrics and ear-shattering rock of the Beatles, Jimi Hendrix, The Who, and Led Zeppelin. . . . Woodstock, the cultural coming-out party of the Boomers, was unlike anything the Builders had ever imagined, much less carried out. Rather than accepting conditions as they were, Boomers questioned everything—until they got the answer they wanted.[3]

If the relationship between the Builders and Boomers was the generation gap, then Barna rightly refers to the relationship between Boomers and Busters as the generational Cold War. Researchers indicate, though, a clear shift in the rising generation of young people. And the relationship between the members of Generation Z, their parents (younger Busters and older Millennials), and youth leaders will be, I believe, essential for the spiritual health of this generation.

Gen Z College Student

Those who study generations have observed a subtle truth in the lives of thousands of teens across America. They look to adults—both family members and spiritual leaders—for real guidance. Groups of college students are in my home on a regular basis, attending small group Bible studies. These small groups are multigenerational. At first, I was shocked that so many college students wanted to attend our life group. I asked one of them why he came to a multigenerational group in our home when there were so many monogenerational groups on

---

3   George Barna, *Real Teens: A Contemporary Snapshot of Youth Culture* (Ventura: Regal, 2001), 13.

our university's campus. He said, "I could ask my roommate how to ask a girl to marry me, but he's never done it. You have. So, I want to learn from adults who have more life experience and wisdom." Teenagers are no different. They want adults to serve as role models and examples of how to live.

These Christ-following members of Generation Z want us to teach them not only to be adults but also to be godly adults. Richard Ross—professor of youth ministry at Southwestern Baptist Theological Seminary and probably the man who knows more youth pastors than anyone else—made this observation:

> The good news is that across the years, hundreds of thousands of teenagers have been introduced to Jesus, discipled, equipped and mobilized for kingdom activity. Most of the adults through whom Christ is extending his kingdom today are a product of local church youth ministries. I join parents, senior pastors, youth pastors and lay leaders in celebrating ministries with teenagers that have carried the aroma of Jesus and have pushed back the darkness.[4]

That piqued my interest, as similar testimonies have been repeated to me by many student pastors and youth.

Thus I am confident about the future. I don't see the world through rose-colored glasses, nor am I a glib optimist who ignores real issues (like youth-ministry challenges). But I'm convinced that God is in control of the universe and that he is living and active in this world.

Daniel of the Old Testament and his three young friends had every reason to collapse—snatched from their home and their homeland while so young, facing the brainwashing Babylonians. But they saw God's work in the midst of that, and so should we.

---

4   Richard Ross, "Time for 'Radical Reevaluation' of Youth Ministry," *Word & Way*, December 11, 2019, https://wordandway.org/2019/12/11/richard-ross-time-for-radical-reevaluation-of-youth-ministry.

The wind of the Spirit blows where it will. We do not tell God what to do. But if we journey with him, we, like good sailors, can set the sails to go with the wind of his Spirit. And a refreshing wind is moving among the youth in our country. God is raising up a new generation. As leaders and parents, we would do well to set the sails in a manner that uplifts this coming generation and helps them to reach their peers with the life-giving gospel of Jesus Christ.

Getting to Know Generation Z

In a letter to the church in Corinth, the apostle Paul wrote:

> For though I am free from all, I have made myself a servant to all, that I might win more of them. To the Jews I became as a Jew, in order to win Jews. To those under the law I became as one under the law (though not being myself under the law) that I might win those under the law. To those outside the law I became as one outside the law (not being outside the law of God but under the law of Christ) that I might win those outside the law. To the weak I became weak, that I might win the weak. I have become all things to all people, that by all means I might save some. I do it all for the sake of the gospel, that I may share with them in its blessings. (1 Cor. 9:19–23)

Paul knew the culture he sought to reach. He bridged the gospel to that culture. He did not change the message but changed the methods and means of evangelism. In so doing, he built bridges to the culture over which the gospel could travel.

If we are going to reach the members of Generation Z with the gospel, we must first know who they are. We need to study their generational characteristics. The following is a list of the key characteristics of Generation Z.

1. They are wired in. Generation Z spends more time on their cell phones, tablets, laptops, and computers than any other generation of students in the country. Because of this prevalent use of technology, Jean Twenge calls Generation Z *iGen*. Her research reveals:

> iGen high school seniors spent just over two hours a day texting on their cell phones, about two hours a day on the Internet, an hour and a half a day on electronic gaming, and about a half hour on video chat in the most recent survey. That totals to six hours a day with new media—and that's just during their leisure time. Eighth graders, still in middle school, were not far behind, spending an hour and a half a day each texting, browsing online, and gaming, and about half an hour on video chat—a total of five hours a day with new media.[5]

Teens spend more time on social media and on their screens than they do in face-to-face interactions with each other. While social media and technology allow teens to interact with a greater variety of people, they do not allow for the depth of interaction that occurs in face-to-face meetings. It's not a surprise then that the more time teens spend on social media, the sadder they are and lonelier they feel. So much screen time causes them to yearn for authentic relationship.

2. They are post-Christian. In the book *Meet Generation Z*, James Emery White asserts, "The most defining characteristic of Generation Z is that it is arguably the first generation in the West (certainly in the United States) that will have been raised in a post-Christian context. As a result, it is the first post-Christian generation."[6] Members of Gen Z do not have a point of reference spiritually to biblical truth. Up until the Millennials, past generations possessed some exposure to the church. Now a larger number of parents and teenagers in America claim no religious affiliation. Professor of psychology at San Diego State University Jean Twenge notes of her research regarding the religious beliefs and activity of Gen Z, "This suggests that two forces are working simultaneously to pull iGen'ers away from reli-

---

5   Jean M. Twenge, *iGen* (New York: Astria, 2017), 51.
6   James Emery White, *Meet Generation Z* (Grand Rapids: Baker, 2017), 49.

gion: more iGen'ers are being raised in nonreligious households, and more iGen teens have decided not to belong to a religion anymore."[7] There is an increase in the number of atheists and agnostics in this generation. Barna notes, "The percentage of Gen Z that identifies as atheist is *double* that of U.S. adults."[8] All of these indicators point to a generation that desperately needs the gospel.

Many in Generation Z, more than in generations before them, are a spiritual blank slate. They are drawn to spiritual things, but their starting point is vastly different from previous generations, many of whom received a basic education on the Bible and Christianity.[9]

3. They struggle with their mental and emotional health. While not totally related to their use of technology, there are more members of Generation Z seeking counseling for mental health and emotional issues than any other generation in history. For example, the number of teenage girls in Generation Z who have considered or attempted suicide increased significantly. This generation also has more members experiencing depressive episodes and feelings of loneliness and unhappiness. While Millennials were generally optimistic about the future, members of Generation Z struggle to find safety, peace, and freedom from anxiety. Barna states, "Between financial crisis and perpetual war, they are apt to be distrustful of the future."[10] In general, they are struggling to find hope for the future.

As Twenge summarizes, "iGen'ers look so happy online, making goofy faces on Snapchat and smiling in their pictures on Instagram. But dig deeper, and reality is not so comforting. iGen is on the verge of the most severe mental health crisis for young people in decades. On the surface, though, everything is fine."[11]

4. They struggle with the issue of identity. Discovering identity is a part of adolescent development; however, the presence of social media and changing views in American culture regarding gender identity

---

7   Twenge, *iGen*, 122.
8   Barna Group, *Gen Z*, 25.
9   Barna Group, *Gen Z*, 26
10 Barna Group, *Gen Z*, 29.
11 Twenge, *iGen*, 93.

present serious challenges for the members of Generation Z. Teens see a false reality on social media. People do not post their worst pictures or videos on social media. They post the most appealing and attractive photos and videos they have. This presentation of reality is a false one. Sadly, it has an impact on teens, who are consuming social media sometimes for hours a day. Teens see a picture of "reality" that simply is not accurate. In addition, they see photos of "friends" at social events to which they were not invited and experience feelings of missing out. All of these aspects of social media impact their perception of themselves—their identity.

Many members of Generation Z also experience confusion about the relationship between gender and identity. The Barna Group found in their research that "only half of today's teens believe one's sex at birth defines one's gender. One-third says gender is 'what a person feels like.' Twelve percent do not know how to answer this question, while smaller percentages say, 'a person's desires or sexual attraction' or 'the way society sees a person.'"[12] Increasingly American society and the media speak of sexual orientation as if it is synonymous with gender identity. These societal changes impact the members of Generation Z in their understanding of identity.

5. They are diverse. Regarding this characteristic of Generation Z, James White notes, "When the 2020 census is conducted, it is estimated that more than half of all US children will be a part of a minority race or ethnic group."[13] Further clarifying the racial make-up of Generation Z, the Barna Group's study reveals, "About half of Gen Z is nonwhite. They are the most racially and ethnically diverse generation in American history."[14] This diversity creates an expectation from Generation Z that other generations and aspects of society, including the church, reflect diversity. As a warning to American churches, Barna cautions, "American churches' overall lack of racial and ethnic diversity could become a major stumbling block for a

---

12 Barna Group, *Gen Z*, 46.
13 White, *Meet Generation Z*, 46.
14 Barna Group, *Gen Z*, 14.

generation that has already begun to see the church as irrelevant to their lives."[15] Diversity is not only a characteristic of the generation but also one of its values. The members of Generation Z are a mosaic people of various races and ethnicities.

6. *They are growing up "too slow" and "too fast."* The members of Generation Z are a paradox. They obtain their driver's licenses at a later age than preceding generations. My oldest sons did not get their licenses until their senior year of high school. Many teens choose to forego getting a driver's license. Jean Twenge asserts that this "decline in driving appears across all regions, ethnic groups, and socioeconomic classes."[16] Because they are not driving, members of Generation Z spend less time hanging out with friends and going on dates. If they do go out, their parents take them.

It's possible that their driving habits, or lack thereof, stem from a desire for safety. Because members of Generation Z experienced the two recessions and the war on terror, they have a desire to feel safe—physically and emotionally. This desire for safety protects them against some harmful activity. They binge-drink less, have less premarital sex, and have lower instances of fighting than previous generations.[17] On the flip side, their value of feeling safe causes them to feel anxiety when faced with ideas or beliefs that oppose theirs or upset their status quo. Such resistance to opposing ideas might stifle their intellectual and spiritual discovery.

At the same time, in some ways, Generation Z is growing up too quickly. This fast pace is especially evident in the area of sexuality. The members of Generation Z are exposed to issues related to sexuality and sexual identity at a younger age then any generation in the history of the nation. James White laments, "No other generation has had pornography so available, in such extremes, at such a young age. Seventy percent of all eighteen- to thirty-four-year-olds are regular

---

15   Barna Group, *Gen Z*, 74.
16   Twenge, *iGen*, 28.
17   Twenge, *iGen*, 146, 150, 206.

viewers. The average age to begin viewing? Eleven."[18] Generation Z also is growing up during a time when very public conversations occur in society regarding same-sex attraction, same-sex relationships, same-sex marriage, transgender lifestyles, and so on. They are likely to see some of these issues played out on television and in movies. So, regarding issues of sexuality, the American society pressures members of Generation Z to grow up too fast.

7. *The parents of Generation Z are both overengaged and underengaged in their parenting.* The Generation X parents of the members of Generation Z often overparent their teens. They micromanage homework rather than helping their children develop time management and study skills. When there is a conflict with a grade on an assignment, often the parent will communicate directly with the teacher rather than encouraging the student to inquire about the grade. Parents sometimes discourage their students from driving and volunteer to drive because they are afraid of their students getting injured in an accident. These examples are just a few of the ways that parents of Generation Z are overengaged.

At the same time, Gen Z's parents permit freedom and a hands-off approach in areas where their students need parental guidance. I mentioned earlier in this chapter the amount of time teens spend in front of media screens. Parents allow their students to use the internet, cell phones, and other technology unmonitored and unrestricted. They often have no filters on their teens devices which could easily restrict their student's access to pornography and harmful web sites. Parents of Gen Z aren't only disengaged regarding technology, but also do not discuss spiritual matters with their students. In a study of students who actively attended church youth groups, researchers found that "only 27 percent of students say their family regularly discussed spiritual things or prayed together."[19] So, parents are engaged when they need to give freedom and disengaged when they need to provide parental guidance.

---

18 White, *Meet Generation Z*, 58.
19 Ben Trueblood, *Within Reach* (Nashville: Lifeway, 2018), 38–39.

8. Gen Z is a generation of entrepreneurs. According to the consulting firm Sparks & Honey, "72% of high school students want to start a business someday (compared to 64% of college students)."[20] I've seen this entrepreneurial spirit in my Gen Z children. My sons started a lawn care business at the age of fifteen. At the same age, one of my sons started a YouTube channel focused on gaming. He was even able to make a little money off of ads on the channel. My daughter made bead jewelry, had business cards printed, and sold her products at a local market in town. Now a college student, my son Noah is currently working on a podcast that he and his peers started to discuss how they can bring their college community together.

9. They are the largest generation in the nation's history. The sheer population of Generation Z indicates their potential for making an impact upon American society. As early as 2014, marketing firms began to conduct research on this generation because of their profitability as consumers in the American economy. Because of their size, media and advertising increasingly focus their attention on this generation. It will be interesting to see the impact they have on the older generations as the American economy increasingly targets this younger audience. In matters of faith, the size of this generation grants them great potential to make an impact for the kingdom of Christ. Imagine the number of missionaries they can send out to their communities and around the world.

10. They are students. The members of Generation Z seek and see the value of education. Sparks & Honey observes, "1 in 2 Gen Zers will be university educated (compared with 1 in 3 for Millennials and 1 in 4 for Gen X)."[21] Having served as a university professor since 2013, I've seen the transition from Millennials in my classroom to members of Gen Z in my classes. I've observed an increase in students' desire to learn and obtain as much knowledge of the fields I

---

20 "Meet Generation Z: Forget Everything You Learned about Millennials," Sparks & Honey, June 17, 2014, https://www.slideshare.net/sparksandhoney/generation-z-final-june-17.

21 "Meet Generation Z."

teach. At the same time, through technology, members of Gen Z have more knowledge at their fingertips than any other generation. They have great potential to make advances in knowledge and education. Because they are learners, they are generally open to hearing about spiritual matters if such truths are presented with intellectual depth.

Even as I described Generation Z, I got excited about the potential this generation has to advance the kingdom of Christ. I am mindful of the numerous ways that bridges to the gospel can be built to members of this generation using the knowledge above. Parents and youth leaders have a tremendous opportunity to have conversations with this generation regarding how the gospel and the Word of God relate to issues of identity, anxiety, racial diversity, mental health, emotional health, the use of time, and a plethora of other connecting points that arise from these dynamics related to Generation Z.

3

THE POTENCY OF EXPECTANCY
WHY WE CAN BE OPTIMISTIC

Now those who were scattered because of the persecution that arose over Stephen traveled as far as Phoenicia and Cyprus and Antioch, speaking the word to no one except Jews. But there were some of them, men of Cyprus and Cyrene, who on coming to Antioch spoke to the Hellenists also, preaching the Lord Jesus. And the hand of the Lord was with them, and a great number who believed turned to the Lord. The report of this came to the ears of the church in Jerusalem, and they sent Barnabas to Antioch. When he came and saw the grace of God, he was glad, and he exhorted them all to remain faithful to the Lord with steadfast purpose, for he was a good man, full of the Holy Spirit and of faith. And a great many people were added to the Lord.

—Acts 11:19–24

Have you ever had a sense of expectancy about something that you hope God is getting ready to do?

Two summers ago I preached a summer camp for a church located on the coast of South Carolina. I'd preached a midweek service for them the previous spring. The church's youth pastor, Jack Powers Jr., communicated with me at least once a month regarding what he was doing to prepare the hearts of the students for camp. He talked with me about the week of camp and what biblical passages he and I would cover in the morning and evening worship services. I sensed Jack's excitement as he celebrated how many students signed up to be a part of the week of camp. We rejoiced together a few weeks before camp that several players from the local high school football team would also join us. Jack graciously invited my family to accompany me and participate in the camp activities along with his students (my twins were seniors, my oldest daughter a junior, and my youngest daughter a sixth grader). Having already had a positive meeting with the students, seeing Jack's spiritual preparation of the group leading up to camp, knowing who would be attending, and anticipating a week with my family in a place where we could focus on the Lord together without distraction, I was excited.

As I drove our minivan down the winding Tennessee backroad that led from the highway hard top to the camp's entrance, I felt a building anticipation that God was about to do something special that week. In the months prior to camp, Jack had focused on the students' spiritual preparation. I prayerfully prepared my messages, thinking about particular students I knew would be at camp and asking the Lord to move in our lives that week. I knew that we could not control the Holy Spirit or manipulate a movement of God, but I just felt that, with all the preparation, we had hoisted the sail to catch the movement of the Spirit. So, as I drove and thought about that evening's worship service, I possessed a hopeful expectation that God was going to move.

And move he did. Starting on the first night of camp, students surrendered their lives to Christ. Every night that week, students responded to the invitation to do God's will in their lives. We saw students become Christ followers, recommit their lives to Christ, make their faith public through the waters of baptism, and answer the call to ministry. That week at camp taught me to never ignore or discourage a hopeful expectancy for God to move when we've done all we can do to hoist the sail to catch the blowing of the Holy Spirit.

I sense the same hopeful expectancy for God to move in Generation Z. I believe there are a number of factors that can give us hope. The sail is being hoisted in several areas related to youth ministry.

The Power of the Gospel and the Potential of Generation Z

When we consider the challenges the members of Generation Z face that I mentioned in chapter 2, we might be tempted to become discouraged. The statistics regarding the mental health of today's teenagers are sobering and disturbing. The stories of students who feel no self-worth or possess an unhealthy understanding of identity because they compare their lives to the false world they experience as they immerse themselves in social media are heartbreaking. Add to that the post-Christian nature of our society, and we may be tempted to throw our hands up and ask, "How can we have hopeful expectancy for Generation Z?"

In rabbinic fashion, because I am a teacher, I respond with these questions: Do we still believe that the gospel of Jesus Christ is good news? Do we still believe in the transformative power of the gospel?

The apostle Paul wrote to a pluralistic Roman culture: "For I am not ashamed of the gospel, for it is the power of God for salvation to everyone who believes, to the Jew first and also to the Greek" (Rom. 1:16). The power of the gospel to save lives has not dissipated since the time of the apostle Paul. Greg Stier writes:

> But Satan whispers in our ears that it's not the same, that Paul's gospel was somehow infused with apostolic superpowers, and that our high-tech, Westernized teenagers are somehow immune to the power of the gospel. He tells us they're too spoiled, too apathetic, and too distracted for the gospel to get through to them. . . . The gospel is as powerful now as it was then, as it ever was, and as it ever will be. And so is the Holy Spirit. He works to convict, convince, and convert the unreached to produce radical gospel transformation.[1]

---

1 Greg Stier, *Gospelize* (Arvada, CO: D2S Publishing, 2015), 32.

When the members of Generation Z encounter Jesus Christ through the good news of the gospel, they begin to obtain a biblical understanding of their identity. They experience hope and peace that eclipses the anxiety and fear with which so many of them struggle. The gospel counters the doubt and lack of purpose so evident in the post-Christian culture in which they live. They also leverage potentially harmful characteristics of their generation and redeem them to the glory of God and the advancement of the gospel.

For example, the gospel transforms how members of Generation Z use technology and media. I met a student from Texas at a camp I preached last summer who uses a website and her Instagram account to post devotionals and poetry she writes to reach and encourage her peers with the gospel and the Word of God. Students use their cell phones to text devotional or encouraging messages to their friends. During Dare 2 Share weekends, Greg Stier encourages students to use their cell phones as a witnessing tool:

> After we train teenagers to share the good news, we have them hold their cell phones up high into the air. And then we have them call or text their friends and initiate a gospel conversation. Many of them give me that "Are you serious?" look as it begins to sink in that I'm actually asking them to do this totally out of their comfort zone thing. . . . But before I have them call or text their friends, we pray. And you can feel the prayers going up, because for many of these teenagers, this is the first time they've been put in a position of risk.[2]

Imagine what could happen when the gospel captures the largest generation in the history of our nation. Think about how God can use the entrepreneurial spirit of the members of Gen Z to advance the gospel in their communities and around the world. They are not afraid to build from nothing.

---

2 Stier, *Gospelize*, 49.

Their spirit is captured by a student I had the privilege of teaching. She had just graduated from high school and completed her first year of college. Rather than spending her summer making money for the next school year, she decided to take the gospel to an island that is part of the largest Muslim country in the world. She spent her summer on that isolated island sharing the gospel with the people there because she knew they had never heard it. Her entrepreneurial kingdom focus is indicative of the Christ followers who are part of her generation. I am hopeful because of how the gospel changes teenagers like her and transforms them into entrepreneurial ambassadors who are willing to take the gospel into their communities or around the world simply because it is not there yet. I agree with Barry St. Clair when he says, "Students have awesome potential to change their world."[3]

The Missional Shift in the Church and in Youth Ministry

The term *missional* is a rather recent invention in the life of the church; however, it is a concept that dates back to the early church. Being missional simply means to approach our communities with the *missio Dei*, or mission of God, in mind and to see our context like a missionary would. When we are acting missionally, we study our culture and its people and seek ways to contextualize the gospel to reach people in our culture and communities. We act incarnationally, adopting the dress, language, music, and food of our culture (within biblical guidelines).

Being missional also involves a *glocal* context. Many church leaders now focus on how their congregations can reach their community while at the same time partnering with missionaries and indigenous Christians in countries that are unreached and/or unengaged with the gospel. The focus on local missions and global missions—*glocal*.

This missional focus impacts student ministries as well. There is a shift in student ministry from an attractional approach to student ministry, characterized by events and an "if you build it, they will

---

3 Barry St. Clair, foreword to Greg Stier, *Outbreak: Creating a Contagious Youth Ministry through Viral Evangelism* (Chicago: Moody, 2002), 10.

come" mentality, to a theology of youth ministry that sees it more as an extension of the missional efforts of the church. Youth make up a particular subculture within a community. They have their own language, dress, and even food that align with their culture. More youth ministers see the students in their community as a local mission field and themselves as missionaries. Missionaries study their culture, lead people in their culture to Christ, disciple these new believers, and send them out to reach their unreached family members and friends. When youth ministries contextualize in this way, they reflect their communities rather than each other. Missional youth ministry by definition does not lend itself to a "cookie cutter" attractional approach.

This missional approach in youth ministry also does not separate the youth group from its local congregation; rather, missional youth groups see themselves as a part of their church's overall missional strategy to reach their communities. Youth in these missional youth groups work with adult leaders, parents, and other adults in the church to engage their communities. Missional youth ministers equip the adult leaders, parents, and students in their ministries to understand the connection between missions in a local and global context. They help their students develop an understanding about how making disciples in their communities and around the world are both part of the *missio Dei*. Rather than an "if you build it, they will come" approach, these youth groups go to unchurched people locally and around the world to engage them with the gospel as part of their church's missions and evangelism strategy. Thus missional youth ministry helps youth groups to avoid becoming a parachurch within their local churches.

This missional focus concentrates on making disciples. The goal is to disciple the adult leaders, parents, and students so that they become mature fruit-bearing church members—fruit bearing as it relates to the fruits of the Spirit as well as the fruit of multiplying other disciples. The scope of the missional strategy is the same scope mentioned by Jesus in Matthew 28:19–20. He told his disciples to make disciples of *panta ta ethne*, people from every tribe, tongue, and nation. Considering the diversity present in the members of Generation Z, they are poised to carry the gospel to people from a wide variety of ethnic backgrounds. In addition, when one considers the sheer size of Generation Z, their potential for kingdom impact is tremendous.

Because of this shift toward a more missional approach to youth ministry and the potential impact that Generation Z possesses, I am hopeful about the future.

The Shift toward the Family in Youth Ministry

In addition to a shift toward a more missional approach to the church, churches also shifted toward an emphasis on the family. Many youth ministers noticed that they segmented students away from the family and the rest of the congregation in their efforts to reach teenagers with the gospel. They also realized that their efforts at youth ministry were actually creating a parachurch group (the youth group) within the congregation. Ministers like Reggie Joiner at North Point Community Church began to realize, "At best, with those who attended our church consistently, we would only have about forty hours in a given year to influence a child."[4] At the same time, church leaders realized that parents more time than anyone else with their students. We youth leaders began to conclude that perhaps one reason we witnessed young adults aged eighteen to twenty-two dropping out of the church is that we had failed to partner with parents and other adults in the church in discipling teenagers.

I'm encouraged by the changes I'm seeing in youth ministry as a response to this refocus on the family. Over the past decade, three primary family ministry approaches surfaced to address this need for parents to disciple their children/teenagers: family-based ministry, family-integrated ministry, and family-equipping ministry.

Mark DeVries introduced family-based ministry with his book bearing that title.[5] He proposed that youth ministers incorporate parents as much as possible in their existing activities. At the time, this

---

4   Reggie Joiner, *Think Orange* (Colorado Springs: David C. Cook, 2009), 85.
5   Mark DeVries, *Family-Based Youth Ministry* (Downers Grove, IL: InterVarsity Press, 2004).

thought was a novel response to the "isolation of teenagers from the adult world and particularly their own parents" as youth ministries detached students from their parents and from the congregation.[6]

Rather than integrate parents into the youth ministry of the church, the family-integrated model proposed that churches not separate youth and children from any of the activities of the church congregation. Describing this approach, proponent Voddie Baucham Jr. wrote, "Our church has no youth ministers, children's ministers, or nursery. We do not divide families into component parts. We do not separate the mature women from the young teenage girls who need their guidance. We do not separate the toddler from his parents during worship. In fact, we don't even do it in Bible study. We see the church as a family of families."[7] So the family-integrated model keeps children and students together with their families in every aspect of the church.

Finally, Timothy Paul Jones introduced the family-equipping model as a way to join youth ministers with parents in discipling students. He defines this approach as the "process of intentionally and persistently coordinating a ministry's proclamation and practices so that parents are acknowledged, trained, and held accountable as primary disciple-makers in their children's lives."[8] Jones advocates that youth ministers come alongside parents to help equip them to disciple their students, understanding that they have more time with their children than any other adults. He contends that families should be gospel-focused and that parents should see their children primarily as potential brothers or sisters in Christ. Jones's approach has a missional flavor, as he sees the family as a hub from which the gospel spreads into communities. He writes, "The essence of family-equipping ministry is the implementation of this gospel-centered identity first in our homes and then beyond our homes. The gospel is to be rehearsed in our

---

6 DeVries, *Family-Based Youth Ministry*, 21.

7 Voddie Baucham Jr., *Family Driven Faith: Doing What It Takes to Raise Sons and Daughters Who Walk with God* (Wheaton, IL: Crossway, 2007), 191.

8 Timothy Paul Jones, *Family Ministry Field Guide* (Indianapolis: Wesleyan, 2011), 33.

homes and reinforced in our churches so that it can be revealed with integrity to the world."[9] Jones also advocates that adults in churches can help spread the gospel by discipling students whose unchurched parents do not attend the church.

Although these three approaches to family ministry vary in their strategies, they hold a common conviction that a focus on families is imperative for healthy ministry to teenagers. They agree that parents are the primary disciplers of their students. These family ministry models also emphasize the importance of students' involvement in intergenerational relationships in the congregation.

I'll talk more about family ministry and how youth leaders and parents can work together in discipling students in part 2. For now, just know that I am extremely hopeful regarding this renewed emphasis upon the family in youth ministry.

Seeing the Potential

What would happen if the largest generation in the history of this nation developed a kingdom vision for the gospel to advance in their communities and around the world? What would happen if families became missional hubs within our churches where children and teenagers are discipled and become disciple-makers of their fellow family members, peers, and acquaintances? What would happen if adults in churches discipled students whose parents are unchurched and those teenagers went back to their homes bearing the good news of the gospel? What would happen if parents developed a missional vision that their sons and daughters would become missionaries to their communities and to unreached people groups overseas?

Can you see the potential?

I look toward the horizon with hopeful expectancy!

---

9 Jones, *Family Ministry Field Guide*, 144.

4

TRUTH OR CONSEQUENCES
BIBLICAL TEACHING CONFRONTS CONTEMPORARY PRACTICE

> And Jesus increased in wisdom and in stature
> and in favor with God and man.
> —Luke 2:52

In *Meet Generation Z*, James Emery White laments that today's teenagers only have an eight-second attention span, which he calls an eight-second filter. He compares this attention span to that of a goldfish—in fact, it is even shorter than that of "Bubbles" the goldfish.[1] While White is correct that members of Generation Z have the ability to filter information very quickly, one might interpret his comparison with Bubbles as negative and pejorative toward teenagers and their ability to focus on information and tasks.

While White's book is helpful at some points in describing this current generation, some might use his comments to promote a misguided notion regarding teenagers' attention spans that ignores the capacity of students to complete class projects, participate in hour-long classes, sit through movies, or spend hours meticulously editing videos on their YouTube channels. Although I believe his intentions are good—the comments he makes about attention spans appear in his section on reaching teenagers with the gospel—White's comments might be interpreted as implying that students do not have the capacity to listen or pay attention to the gospel for lon-

---

1 James Emery White, *Meet Generation Z* (Grand Rapids: Baker Books, 2017), 113–14.

ger than eight seconds unless it is presented in a flashy way using multimedia.

My experience preaching to members of Generation Z does not support White's conclusions. I've observed, with joy, sixth- through twelfth-graders paying attention to thirty-five-minute sermons I've preached at various summer camps. They did not listen because I presented a multimedia display (all I had was my voice and the Bible). They listened because of the power of the Holy Spirit working through the Word being preached. We must be careful in our discussion of the attention spans of Generation Z not to show contempt toward the power of the Holy Spirit, the Word of God, or the place of preaching in the Christian church. We should also avoid treating students like children who, through the influence of media and social media, cannot pay attention; they are young adults who are capable of focusing.

As a matter of fact, history records stirring examples of young people serving the Lord and showing great spiritual maturity, but the church today has not taken seriously the need to equip students theologically. This failure has led to underchallenged and undertrained youth. Many studies demonstrate a further change from past generations: the erosion of theological conviction among college students in evangelical schools.[2]

A Biblical Perspective: The Myth of Adolescence

Greek scholar David Alan Black allowed the use the title of his book *The Myth of Adolescence* to make this point. "What," Black asks, "do the Scriptures say about adolescence? *Absolutely* nothing."[3] Moses, Paul, John, and others went from childhood to adulthood. Were they ever teenagers? Yes. But they were never adolescents. Black argues that, biblically, there are three stages to one's life:

---

2 Alvin L. Reid, "From Northampton to Columbine: Understanding the Potential of Young People for the Contemporary Church," address to the Evangelical Theological Society, Colorado Springs, November 14, 2001.

3 David Alan Black, *The Myth of Adolescence* (Yorba Linda, CA: Davidson, 1998), 19.

1. Childhood/pre-adulthood (ages one to twelve)
2. Emerging adulthood (ages twelve to thirty)
3. Senior adulthood (age thirty to death)[4]

Black notes that these stages can be seen in the life of Jesus (Luke 2:41–52; 3:23; and the remainder of the gospel, respectively) and in the persons John describes in his first epistle ("little children," "young people," and "fathers"). The transitions are significant: puberty at age twelve, and the move to responsible adulthood at about age thirty. Notice the absence of a separate category of teenage years.

The Old Testament denotes other categories. In the Pentateuch, for example, men twenty and older were fit for war (see Num. 26), and only those twenty and older could give an offering (Exod. 30:14). While these and other distinctives are found in the Old Covenant, Black's argument stands: the Bible mentions nothing of the separate place of the teen years. Nor does it mention the concomitant expectation of adolescent behavior, which expectation is so prevalent in American culture, including in the church.

Black argues, and I would agree, that there's no biblical warrant for the concept of adolescence. Yet that concept has led to an entire subculture of youth ministry—well-intentioned but too often poorly founded—as well as the remarkable growth of so-called family ministries in the church.

> According to the Bible, the teen era is not a "time-out" between childhood and adulthood. It is not primarily a time of horseplay. . . . The Bible treats teens as responsible adults, and so should we. Paul told Timothy, a young man, "Don't let anyone look down on you because you are young. Instead, be an example for other believers in your speech, behavior, love, faith, and purity" (1 Tim. 4:12).[5]

---

4 Black, *Myth of Adolescence*, 6.
5 Black, *Myth of Adolescence*, 22.

Does this mean youth are to be prohibited from enjoying times of innocent, carefree play? Certainly not. But the idea of suspending life for a multiyear period of silliness is . . . well . . . silliness.

The concept of adolescence has led our culture, both inside and outside the church, to fabricate two myths about youth. First, it encourages teenagers to behave like grade-school children instead of young adults. Second, it perpetuates the notion that the teenage years are, of necessity, a time of rebellion, sarcasm, narcissism, and general evildoing. "Sowing wild oats" has become a popular term for what is expected of youth—including churched youth—during their young adult days. Certainly, the hormonal changes and rapid maturation taking place in adolescence may, if left unchecked, result in such behavior. But that's my point: we must not let the bar of expectation be set so low.

More and more voices are sounding a challenge to the notion of adolescence. Soon after Columbine, *Time* magazine featured a back-page article that calls into question the way society as a whole has treated young people in recent generations. Lance Morrow observes,

> Humans . . . have turned the long stretch from puberty to autonomy into a suspended state of simultaneous overindulgence and neglect. American adolescence tends to be disconnected from the adult world and from the functioning expectation . . . of entering that world and assuming a responsible place there. The word *adolescence* means, literally, growing up. No growing up occurs if there is nothing to grow up to. Without the adult connection, adolescence becomes a Neverland, a Mall of Lost Children.[6]

In the *Time* article, Morrow referred to an op-ed piece by Leon Botstein, president of Bard College, that appeared the week before in *The New York Times*. Botstein suggested, "The American High School

---

6 Lance Morrow, "The Boys and Bees: The Shootings Are One More Argument for Abolishing Adolescence," *Time*, May 31, 1999, 110.

is obsolete and should be abolished." Morrow added, "At sixteen, young Americans are prepared to be taken seriously. . . . They need to enter a world where they are not in a lunchroom only with their peers." Morrow then offers a fascinating opinion coming from the mainstream, secular media:

> Maybe we should abolish adolescence altogether. Not the biological part. . . . We are stuck with that. But it would be nice if we could get rid of the cultural mess we have made of the teenage years. Having deprived children of an innocent childhood, the least we would do is rescue them from an adolescence corrupted by every sleazy, violent and commercially lucrative fantasy that untrammeled adult venality, high-horsing on the First Amendment, can conceive.[7]

Morrow notes a scene in J. D. Salinger's *Catcher in the Rye* (1951)—a book he calls "one of the founding documents of American adolescence." Holden Caulfield is a young man who was expelled from a prep school. After donning a red hat, Caulfield was asked by a kid whether it was a deer-shooting hat. Squinting as if aiming to shoot, Caulfield replied, "This is a people shooting hat. I shoot people in it."[8] A generation later, life has imitated art.

Black cites an article by David Bakan that notes three origins of adolescence theory. First, compulsory education laws were passed that changed the centuries-old process of parents teaching their children, putting education into the hands of the state. Second, child labor laws were passed that made it illegal for persons to work before a certain age. While aimed no doubt at protecting children, the laws served to take away responsibilities from many who were ready to take them. Finally, the juvenile justice system was created to separate

---

7   Morrow, "The Boys and Bees," 110.
8   Morrow, "The Boys and Bees," 110.

younger lawbreakers from older ones.[9] Thus, the twentieth century saw the rise of adolescence, accompanied by a plethora of supporting organizations: public schools, Boy Scouts and Girl Scouts, boys' and girls' agricultural clubs, and youth ministry. Black's summation of the results is telling:

> It is my conviction that the social theory of adolescence undermines both the Christian understanding of human nature and the way in which Christians analyze moral thought. [That theory] underscores the modern disinclination to treat a person as responsible for his or her actions. When we assert the "fact" that children are to act like children rather than like adults, [theory] becomes a self-fulfilling prophecy.[10]

The twenty-first century is witnessing a further extension of adolescence. This age category continues to broaden, with college-aged students considered as adolescents because they have not yet begun to *#adult*. It is a pretty well-known fact that the average video-game purchaser is a male in his early thirties. In addition, teenagers are taking a longer time to grow up. Regarding this trend, Jean Twenge writes:

> Thirteen-year-olds—and even eighteen-year-olds—are less likely to act like adults and spend their time like adults. They are more likely, instead, to act like children—not being immature, necessarily, but by postponing the usual activities of adults. Adolescence is now an extension of childhood rather than the beginning of adulthood.[11]

While there are obvious differences between someone who is fifteen and someone who is twenty-five, I agree with Black that teens

---

9   David Bakan, "Adolescence in America: From Idea to Social Fact," *Daedalus* (1971): 979–95, cited in Black, *Myth of Adolescence*, 15.

10   Black, *Myth of Adolesence*, 17.

11   Jean Twenge, *iGen* (New York: Atria, 2017), 41.

can be responsible young adults if given the chance. Further, they can be prepared to be used by God while still in their teens. If teens can learn trigonometry, calculus, and advanced chemistry, then they can learn theology!

As Black maintains, then, the Bible issues no warrant for the concept of adolescence. And, as he further notes, the concept has obviously not worked. What, then, does the Bible say about youth?

Biblical Models

While the Bible does not consign youth to a separate adolescent category as is done today, it does speak often about young adults. A reading of the entire Bible with an eye to what it says about youth finds that the vast majority of references to youth depicts them in a positive light. Certainly the young men mocking Elisha, the youths who give bad advice to Rehoboam, and Eli's wicked sons are negative examples, but these few examples pale in comparison to the many godly, noble, and often heroic youth.

Joseph. As a seventeen-year-old, Joseph's family sold him into slavery; the wife of the man (Potiphar) who showed Joseph kindness tried to seduce him; he wound up in jail because he said no; others abused him and victimized him. Yet Joseph continued to trust God, and God used Joseph to preserve his people. Knowing his people would face tremendous famine in the future, God used the tragic circumstances of a seventeen-year-old. God moved Joseph into a place of leadership, where he provided for Israel when, years later, a famine came.

Samuel. At a time when the voice of God was rare, the boy Samuel heard the voice of God. God saw that the sons of Eli the priest were evil, unfit to continue to minister to the Lord. At that time God heard the cries of a barren woman named Hannah and gave her a son, whom she named Samuel. Samuel would become one of the great spiritual leaders.

David. When King Saul proved unfit as a leader, God took a shepherd boy named David and made him a great king.

I could cite the examples of Esther, Daniel and his friends, Rhoda, and Timothy. And let us not overlook even our Lord. Remember the first recorded words of Jesus? "I must be about my Father's business." That's a good standard for anyone. His age at the time? He was twelve!

The Bible clarifies what we have overlooked—God uses youth. He is sovereign over the universe and knows tomorrow's headlines *yesterday.* Even youth leaders forget this at times. Imagine, then, what great things those headlines of tomorrow might say about the youth of today. The time is ripe to remember Jesus's standard and to lead students to be about the Father's business.

5

ENTERTAINING CHILDREN OR ASSEMBLING AN ARMY?
LESSONS FROM HISTORY

But my servant Caleb, because he has a different
spirit and has followed me fully, I will bring into
the land into which he went, and his descendants
shall possess it.

—Numbers 14:24

Shout. Show. Shove. Shoot.

These were the rules of engagement and steps for escalation in
force that my soldiers carried when we deployed on Operation
Noble Eagle and Operation Enduring Freedom from 2001 to
2002. We were an infantry battalion originally tasked with securing
American facilities and personnel in the United States and later in
Europe as a response to the threat of al-Qaeda after September 11,
2001. My soldiers faced the threat of vehicle-borne improvised explosive devices—tanker trucks or semis rigged with explosives or chemical weapons. There also existed the possibility that individuals might
attack checkpoints or points in the perimeter on foot, using explosives
or small-arms weapons. To counter this threat my infantry soldiers
carried live ammo in their weapons locked and loaded (meaning they
had a round ready to fire in the chamber). Because they carried live
rounds, it was imperative that these infantrymen follow closely the
rules of engagement and the steps for escalation of force issued by
their commanders. While in Europe, their failure to observe the rules
of engagement would ignite an international incident.

Here's the catch, many of these infantry soldiers were eighteen and nineteen years old. Some had recently graduated from high school. The Army and the officers in command required these teenagers to make very adult decisions. The decisions they made would determine life or death for numerous people around them. One wrong decision could be fatal. Yet these infantry troops succeeded in protecting the American soldiers and family members left in their charge.

The United States Army clearly knows something the church has missed: you can lean on young people to respond correctly, even heroically, in high-pressure situations. The church, however, has forgotten this truth.

If We Don't Learn from History, We Will Repeat Its Mistakes

Writer and philosopher George Santayana offers some sage advice: those who fail to learn from history are doomed to repeat its failures. The same advice is offered here, but with a twist: those who fail to note the impact of youth in history are doomed to miss the potential of youth today.

As noted, the most remarkable, God-driven spiritual awakenings are often inspired by young people. In some cases, the maturity of the seasoned has channeled the zeal of youth into leadership. Jonathan Edwards, J. Edwin Orr, and other historians of awakening have noted the vital role of young people in great revival. We must recapture this understanding today!

Looking to biblical history one also notes shifts in generational attitudes. Prior to entering the Promised Land, for example, an entire generation abandoned faith and died in the wilderness. A new era unfolded, however, with the children of Israel's entrance into the land. Only Joshua and Caleb represented the previous generation. The book of Numbers gives insight into why Caleb was allowed to enter the Promised Land. Caleb had, of course, given a good report, as did Joshua, when both were included in the original party of spies. But Numbers 14:24 adds this insight: "But my servant Caleb, because he had a different spirit in him and has followed me fully,

I will bring into the land where he went, and his descendants shall inherit it."

Little wonder, then, that the psalmist charged elders to teach the coming generation to follow the Lord (Ps. 78:1–7). From his youth, Caleb (and by inference Joshua) was instilled with a "different spirit" from that of the rest of his generation.

Generation Z certainly has a different spirit—not necessarily one that follows the Lord as did Caleb, but one that marks a clear departure from those before it. Generations of youth between Caleb and Millennials have also been marked by a different spirit.

Historically: The Zeal of Youth

Paul told Timothy not to let anyone look down on him because of his youth. But that's not all he said. He exhorted Timothy to *be an example* in speech (a strong argument against a separate youth "lingo"), in behavior, love, faith, and purity (1 Tim. 4:12). Paul apparently believed a young man could be a leader.

As stated earlier, the most overlooked aspect of modern revival movements or awakenings is the role played by young people. Recall that Jonathan Edwards recorded on more than one occasion that the First Great Awakening was, more than anything, a youth movement. Yet in most cases, while the primary sources of history tend to convey one message, the role of youth has been neglected in secondary sources of history.

Pietism

Pietism was a late seventeenth-century reform movement beginning in the Lutheran Church and spreading to other groups. After the Reformation many Lutheran churches became spiritually dead. Thus, some, like Philipp Spener, sought to reform the church, and young people played no small role. Most historians date the beginning of Pietism with the publication of Spener's *Pia Desideria* ("Pious Desires") in 1675.[1] Spener, called the father of Pietism by many,

---

1   Philipp Spener, *Pia Desideria* (1675); Fortress Press continues to publish the book, illustrating its status as a classic in Christian spirituality.

emphasized the personal nature of the Christian experience. He led many small-group Bible studies that spread across parts of Europe, and many young people attended the meetings.

Young people, too, at university helped spread the fervor of Pietism. Spener secured the appointment of A. H. Francke at the new University of Halle in 1692. Under Francke's leadership Halle became "a pietistic center of higher education and revivalism."[2] Francke not only taught theology, but he took the young people out into the community to do hands-on ministry.

Nikolaus Ludwig Von Zinzendorf (1700–1760) studied at Halle from 1710 to 1716. Zinzendorf organized prayer groups among the students while at the university.[3] From Halle, Zinzendorf went to the University of Wittenberg, where in 1718 he formed the Order of the Grain of Mustard Seed. In 1722 he acquired an estate that became a safe haven for persecuted members of the Hussite church. It was from this group that the "Unitas Fratrum" (Unity of the Brethren), or Moravians, was born. A particularly powerful movement of the Spirit came at a communion service on August 12, 1727. Following this, a continuous prayer structure developed, resulting in a missionary enterprise that saw one in every sixty Moravians becoming a missionary. Clearly, Zinzendorf's impact was significant and can be traced to his teen years at Halle.

The Evangelical Awakening in England

John Wesley (1703–1791) and George Whitefield (1714–1770) were two leaders of the Evangelical Awakening in England during the eighteenth century.[4] Wesley's experience as a college student at Oxford

---

2 Earl E. Cairns, *An Endless Line of Splendor: Revivals and their Leaders from the Great Awakening to the Present* (Wheaton, IL: Tyndale House, 1986), 34.

3 See David Howard, "Student Power in World Missions," in *Perspectives on the World Christian Movement*, ed. Ralph Winter (Pasadena, CA: William Carey, 1981), 211–14.

4 For more about the Great Awakenings, see Malcolm McDow and Alvin L. Reid, *Firefall: How God Shaped History through Revivals* (Enumclaw, WA: Pleasant Word, 2002). For information on youth in the history of revival, see

is probably best remembered by the "Holy Club," which involved John, his brother Charles Wesley, Whitefield, and a handful of others. Whitefield was converted during those days. That John Wesley was not actually converted until years after his Oxford days does not minimize the impact made by the Holy Club on his subsequent ministry.

The Holy Club experience forged relationships between the young men, who later figured prominently in the awakening in England and the American colonies. Wesley's often-cited conversion in 1738 led to a remarkable ministry, which, along with Whitefield's influence and Charles's hymn-writing, affected the spiritual life of the entire nation. While never desiring to sever ties with the Church of England, the Evangelical Awakening resulted in the formation of the Methodist Church. By 1791, the year of John Wesley's death, 79,000 Methodist churches had been established in England.

Its Spread to the New World

Beyond his impact in England, Whitefield made seven trips to the New World. His itinerant ministry across the colonies helped to fan the flames of local revivals into the inferno of the Great Awakening. What makes Whitefield's influence more impressive is that he was only twenty-six years old when the Great Awakening was at its peak.

The first of a series of revival movements during the course of Jonathan Edwards's Northampton ministry was the Valley Revival of 1734–1735. Edwards referred to the role of the youth in its origin: "At the latter end of the year 1733, there appeared a very unusual flexibleness, and yielding to advice, in our young people."[5] This came after Edwards began speaking against their irreverence toward the

---

Alvin L. Reid, *Light the Fire: Raising Up a Generation to Live Radically for Jesus* (Enumclaw, WA: Winepress, 2000).

5 Jonathan Edwards, "A Faithful Narrative of the Surprising Work of God, in the Conversion of Many Hundred Souls, in Northampton, and the Neighbouring Towns and Villages of New Hampshire, in New England; in a Letter to the Rev. Dr. Colman, of Boston," in *The Works of Jonathan Edwards*, 2 vols., ed. Sereno E. Dwight (1834; repr., London: Banner of Truth Trust, n.d.), 1:347.

Sabbath. At the same time youth were also greatly affected by the sudden death of a young man and then of a young married woman in their town. Edwards, recognizing an opportunity to change young hearts, proposed that the young people should begin meeting in small groups around Northampton. They did so with such success that many adults followed their example.

Edwards stressed that awakenings were not only inspired and led by young people, they particularly affected the younger generation. Speaking about the effect of the First Great Awakening on youth, he wrote, "God made it, I suppose, the greatest occasion of awakening to others, of anything that ever came to pass in the town. News of it seemed to be almost like a flash of lightning, upon the hearts of young people, all over town, and upon many others."[6] This revival, which erupted in his town of Northampton, Massachusetts, spread quickly to neighboring towns and greatly affected all.

Beyond the impact the awakening had on young people, it must be noted that most of the leaders of the revival were touched by God personally while young. Edwards himself while still a child began his passionate pursuit of God, and his precocious spiritual zeal was obvious in his teen years. The First Great Awakening would include the work of George Whitefield, too, in his twenties at the height of his influence. Several leaders in the First Great Awakening arose from the Log College of Presbyterian William Tennent. Tennent's log house, built to provide ministerial training for three of his sons and fifteen others, made no small mark on the leadership development of ministers during the awakening.[7] After visiting the Tennent family in Pennsylvania, George Whitefield recorded the following in his journal:

> The place wherein the young men study now is in contempt called The College. It is a log house, about twenty feet long and near as many broad; and to me it seemed to resemble

---

6   Edwards, "Faithful Narrative," 1:347.
7   See W. W. Sweet, *The Story of Religion in America* (New York: Harper and Brothers, 1930), 140.

the school of the old prophets, for their habitations were mean. . . . From this despised place, seven or eight worthy ministers of Jesus have lately been sent forth; more are almost ready to be sent, and the foundation is now laying for the instruction of many others.[8]

Leaders from The College in the First Great Awakening included Tenant's sons Gilbert—the most prominent revival leader among Presbyterians—John, and William Jr., along with Samuel Blair. In addition, many graduates established log colleges of their own. The Log College, which ultimately evolved into the College of New Jersey (now Princeton University), has been called "the forerunner of modern seminaries."[9]

At the turn of the nineteenth century the Second Great Awakening spread across the emerging United States. A major precipitating factor in this movement was the outbreak of revival on college campuses. Skepticism and infidelity, influenced by European thinkers, characterized especially eastern colleges during this period immediately following the birth of the United States.

The campus of Hampden-Sydney College in Virginia experienced the first in a series of college revivals, and the fertile field of young students played a pivotal role. Four young men—William Hill, Carey Allen, James Blythe, and Clement Read—were instrumental in the beginnings of revival at Hampden-Sydney in 1787 and the years following. Because they feared severe antagonism from the irreligious student body, the four young men began meeting secretly in the forest to pray and study. When they were discovered, they were greatly ridiculed by fellow students.

Note, though, what happened when John Blair Smith provided appropriate guidance. Smith, the college president, heard of the

---

8 George Whitefield, *The Journals of George Whitefield* (Edinburgh: Banner of Truth, 1960), 354. For more on George Whitefield's theology and methodology of evangelism, see Tim McKnight, *No Better Gospel: George Whitefield's Theology and Methodology of Evangelism* (Timmonsville, SC: Seed, 2017).

9 Earle Cairns, *Endless Line of Splendor* (Wheaton, IL: Tyndale House, 1982), 42.

situation and was convicted by the infidelity on the campus. He invited the four students and others to pray with him in his parlor, arguably an instance of youth ministry. Before long, revival spread rapidly through the college and to surrounding counties. Hill later chronicled the revival's impact:

> Persons of all ranks in society, of all ages . . . became subjects of this work, so that there was scarcely a Magistrate on the bench, or a lawyer at the bar but became members of the church. . . . It was now as rare a thing to find one who was not religious, as it was formerly to find one that was. *The frivolities and amusements once so prevalent were all abandoned, and gave place to singing, serious conversations, and prayer meetings.*[10]

In addition, subsequent revival movements came in 1802, 1814–1815, 1822, 1827–1828, 1831, 1833, and 1837.[11]

The Yale College revival began under the leadership of President Timothy Dwight, the grandson of Jonathan Edwards. When Dwight came to Yale, it was filled with infidelity. He began to preach against unbelief in the college chapel, and by 1797 a group of students formed to improve moral conditions. After much prayer, a powerful spiritual movement permeated the school in the spring of 1802. A third of the student body was converted, and Goodrich wrote of the change in attitude on campus: "The salvation of the soul was the great subject of thought, of conversation, of absorbing interest; the convictions of many were pungent and overwhelming; and 'the peace of believing' which succeeded, was not less strongly marked."[12] The movement spread to Dartmouth and Princeton, at Princeton

---

10 Quoted from Hill's biography in Arthur Dicken Thomas Jr., "Reasonable Revivalism: Presbyterian Evangelization of Educated Virginians, 1787–1837," *Journal of Presbyterian History* 61 (Fall 1983): 322, emphasis added.

11 Thomas, "Reasonable Revivalism," 322.

12 See Chauncy A. Goodrich, "Narrative of Revivals of Religion in Yale College," *American Quarterly Register* 10 (February 1838): 295–96.

three-fourths of the students making professions and one-fourth entering the ministry.[13]

A group of students at Williams College in Massachusetts made a tremendous impact on missions. Samuel Mills entered the college during a time of awakening there between 1804 and 1806. He and four others began to pray regularly for missions, and in 1806 at one particular meeting they had to seek refuge from the rain in a haystack. During this "Haystack Meeting," Mills proposed a mission to Asia; the proposal became a precipitating factor leading to a major foreign missions enterprise. The first missionaries included Adoniram Judson and Luther Rice.[14]

Beyond the colleges, revival began in Northington, Connecticut, with meetings initiated by young people. Bennett Tyler was a sophomore at Yale in 1802 and powerfully impressed by the revival there. He later gathered twenty-five accounts of revival by pastors in New England. In those accounts, no less than twenty emphasized the role of youth in the movements. Revivals on college campuses have continued until today.[15]

Prayer Revival

The Prayer Revival of 1857–1858 was characterized by its wide appeal. Several colleges experienced revival during this time. J. Edwin Orr documented revival movements at Oberlin, Yale, Dartmouth, Middlebury, Williams, Amherst, Princeton, and Baylor.[16] One pivotal feature of this revival in relation to young people was the bearing it

---

13   Goodrich, "Narrative of Revivals," 295–96.
14   See Gardiner Spring, *Memoir of Samuel John Mills* (Boston: Perkins and Marvin, 1829) and Thomas Richards, *Samuel J. Mills: Missionary Pathfinder, Pioneer, and Promoter* (Boston: Pilgrim, 2006).
15   See Bennett Tyler, ed., *New England Revivals, as They Existed at the Close of the Eighteenth Century, and the Beginning of the Nineteenth Centuries* (Wheaton, IL: Richard Owen Roberts, 1980); J. Edwin Orr, *Campus Aflame* (Wheaton, IL: International Awakening, 1992); and John Avant, Malcolm McDow, and Alvin L. Reid, *Revival: An Account of the Current Revival in Brownwood, Fort Worth, Wheaton and Beyond* (Nashville: Broadman and Holman, 1995).
16   J. Edwin Orr, *Fervent Prayer* (Chicago: Moody, 1974), 11–12.

had on twenty-year-old Dwight Lyman Moody. In 1857 Moody wrote of his impression of what was occurring in Chicago: "There is a great revival of religion in this city. . . . [It] seems as if God were here himself."[17] Biographer John Pollock wrote that "the revival of early 1857 tossed Moody out of his complacent view of religion."[18] Moody went on to make a marked impact for Christ during the rest of the nineteenth century.

An aspect of Moody's influence in regard to students that cannot be overlooked was his leadership in the Student Volunteer Movement. Although this movement's roots have been traced ultimately to the Second Great Awakening and the Haystack Meeting of 1806, it was Moody who in 1886 invited 251 students in Mount Hermon, Massachusetts, for a conference. As a result of these meetings, which were highlighted by A. T. Pierson's challenging address, one hundred students volunteered for overseas missions. In 1888 the Student Volunteer Movement was formally organized, with John R. Mott named chairman. Over the next several decades literally thousands of students went to serve as foreign missionaries.

The Twentieth Century

At the turn of the twentieth century, fresh winds of the Spirit again created new movements. These include the Welsh Revival—as well as other developments in the United States and abroad—the birth of modern-day Pentecostalism in 1901 and the subsequent Azusa Street revival. It is interesting to note Charles Parham's influence: one of the key occurrences in the outbreak of Pentecostalism involved students at a Bible school that Charles Parham began in Topeka, Kansas, in 1900; W. J. Seymour, the black pastor who was the catalyst for the Azusa Street revival in Los Angeles, was influenced greatly in 1905 at another Bible school in Houston set up by Parham.

The Welsh Revival concerns specifically the movement that began in 1904 in the tiny country of Wales. A key place of origin of that

---

17   John Pollock, *Moody* (Chicago: Moody, 1983), 34.
18   Pollock, *Moody*, 34.

movement was a church in New Quay, Cardiganshire, where Joseph Jenkins was pastor. During a service, Jenkins asked for personal testimony in response to the question, "What does Jesus mean to you?" A young person, fifteen-year-old Florrie Evans, only recently converted, rose and said, "If no one else will, then I must say that I love the Lord Jesus with all my heart."

Her simple testimony caused many to begin openly surrendering all to Christ, and the fires of revival burned. The revival spread as young people went from church to church, testifying. Itinerant preacher Seth Joshua came to New Quay to speak and was powerfully impressed by the power of God evident there. He then journeyed to speak at Newcastle Emlyn College, and the next week he spoke at nearby Blaenannerch.

A young coal miner named Evan Roberts, who was a ministerial student at Blaenannerch, experienced a powerful personal revival. He felt convicted to return to his home church to address the youth there. Seventeen heard him following a Monday service, he continued preaching, and revival began there.

The revival spread across the country, and news of the awakening spread worldwide. Colleges reported revival, including Denison University in Ohio. Incidentally, it was during this period that Southwestern Baptist Theological Seminary was born.

Throughout the twentieth century, college campuses were a furnace for the flames of revival among youth. From Wheaton to Bethel to Asbury colleges, student revivals seemed to result in a spiritual chemical reaction, blessed in the laboratory of a sovereign God. Is your youth ministry, as it's practiced now, ready for the same chemistry? Is your church willing to be the next laboratory for revival? Do you want to see your family experience revival? Are you ready to help it happen?

6

FROM THE PARACHURCH TO THE LOCAL CHURCH
A BRIEF HISTORY OF YOUTH MINISTRY

> Now when they saw the boldness of Peter and
> John, and perceived that they were uneducated,
> common men, they were astonished. And they
> recognized that they had been with Jesus.
>
> —Acts 4:13

I sat with other youth ministers, youth-ministry volunteers, and summer youth missionaries listening to a youth-ministry "guru" talk about how we needed to do youth ministry. It was interesting to me that every "tip" that he presented related to a particular product his youth ministry group happened to sell, at a discounted rate to the seminar attendees of course. We heard about games in a box, discipleship in a box, missions in a box, calendaring in a box, devotionals in a box, Bible studies in a box, and Jesus in a box (no, I'm just kidding about that one). It was the summer of 1990, and I was getting ready to work as a program director at an interdenominational youth camp. The camp director sent me to the seminar to get new ideas on how to do youth ministry that summer. My nineteen-year-old mind soaked everything up, and I bought it hook, line, and sinker.

During this era of youth-ministry history, youth ministry was seen as a series of attractional events one scheduled on the calendar. The emphasis was on growing the largest youth group possible. Youth were segregated from the church into parachurch groups within congregations that were detached from every other age group in the church. The emphasis was on being fun, cool, and trendy in youth ministry. While leaders of this era mentioned evangelism and discipleship, they measured success in each of these areas by the number of attendees at their events rather than the number of mature Christ followers graduating from their youth groups.

How did we get to that point in youth ministry? In this chapter, I'll take a few moments to give a general survey of the history of youth ministry. While I could go back further in history, my survey will focus upon the 1940s to the present.

The Beginning of Parachurch Youth Ministry

In the late '40s and '50s, teenage culture changed dramatically. The Second World War made an impression upon the generation as they saw older peers go off to war and sometimes not come home. Those service members who went away came back with stories about countries of which teenagers had only read. They had a bigger perspective because of their experience overseas. In addition, teens began to listen to a new style of music that was called rock 'n' roll. Society began to see teen rebellion as a somewhat normal part of growing up. Rebels like James Dean played out this perceived reality on the silver screen.

During this time, churches still approached students from an educational platform. They aimed to teach students about the Bible in Sunday school classes and church services. Churches largely did nothing to change their approach to the changing youth culture. They did not contextualize the gospel to reach the students in their communities.

Several evangelicals who possessed a heart for reaching youth around the nation and the world saw the church's failure to reach the youth in their communities. Regarding this era of youth ministry, Mark Oestreicher writes:

> Churches, in general, were slow to respond to the rise of youth culture (big shock). Churches and church leaders equated youth culture with sinful activities or—at least—unwholesome activities and rebellious attitudes. So those

early youth ministry pioneers who knew they had to be true
to their calling found—in large measure—that they had to
do youth ministry outside the context of the local church.[1]

Evangelicals started organizations like Youth for Christ to engage
students with the gospel. The founders of YFC listed four goals for
the organization:

1. To promote and help win youth for Christ everywhere.
2. To encourage evangelism everywhere.
3. To emphasize radiant, victorious living.
4. To foster international service of youth through existing agencies.[2]

They organized big youth rallies in cities, involving celebrities,
athletes, and musicians to communicate the gospel with teenagers.
YFC enlisted a young man from North Carolina, Billy Graham, as
their primary preacher at these events. Thousands of youth attended
these rallies and thousands came to Christ through them.

This era in youth ministry magnified the contrast between two
different approaches to youth ministry. Churches emphasized more
of an education approach, while parachurch organizations focused
on a more evangelistic approach. The parachurch movements and
rallies that began during this era would have an impact upon how
local churches envisioned youth ministry in the coming years.

The Jesus Movement

The Jesus Movement of the late 1960s and early 1970s touched a
significant number of Baby Boomers. Hippies turned to Christ and
baptized their music, resulting in the revolution known as contempo-

---

1 Mark Oestreicher, *Youth Ministry 3.0* (Grand Rapids: Zondervan, 2008), 46.
2 Mark W. Cannister, "Youth Ministry's Historical Context: The Education
   and Evangelism of Young People," in *Starting Right* (Grand Rapids: Zondervan, 2001), 88.

rary Christian music (CCM); college revivals took hold in places like Asbury in 1970; through youth musicals (*Good News, Tell It Like It Is,* and *Celebrate Life*) and Explo '72 in Dallas, Texas, churches began to see more young faces; seminaries witnessed a huge influx of students. The Jesus Movement touched a generation of evangelicals. Today, many leaders among various denominational and parachurch groups are at some level products of the Jesus Movement. Examples include:

- hundreds, even thousands, of youth choir tours on mission across America singing *Good News, Celebrate Life,* or a similar score;
- drug-laced teens in California and elsewhere taking the eternal trip offered in the gospel;
- churches strengthened: in the Southern Baptist Convention alone, baptisms surpassed 400,000 for five years in a row—the only time this has ever happened (and the biggest percentage of youth baptisms ever);
- a generation of believers touched by the Spirit of God, many of whom now are leading the cry for revival in our time;
- the rise of CCM and the development of praise and worship music in churches;
- an explosion of megachurches, many of which can be traced directly to the Jesus Movement;
- perhaps most significant, a zealous commitment by multitudes of youth to share Christ one on one.

A Youth-Centered Revival

The Jesus Movement touched the youth population almost exclusively, especially appealing to young people outside the established church. While the Jesus Movement is best known for the street Christians who teemed the coastal cities of California in the late 1960s and early 1970s, they were only part of a larger movement of the Spirit. Traditional churches, parachurch groups, and evangelical schools were also touched by the Jesus Movement. I will spend a good bit of time on this movement because it's not really mentioned much in youth ministry historical summaries.

The nonestablishment Jesus People were the most recognizable persons involved in the movement. "Jesus Freaks," *Time* magazine called them—"Evangelical hippies." Or, as many prefer to be called, "street Christians." Duane Pederson coined the terms "Jesus People" and "Jesus Movement,"[3] but "under different names . . . they are the latest incarnation of that oldest of Christian phenomena: footloose, passionate bearers of the Word."[4]

The Jesus Movement, though, spread beyond the Jesus Freaks who came out of the hippie or drug scene. "In associating the Jesus Movement with such a narrow group," Knight argued, "one misses the national pattern of the religious phenomena, which [touched] in one way or another most of the youth of the nation, those still at home, in school and out."[5]

Pederson agreed: "Though the Movement started as a ministry to the street people, it is much wider than that now. It is reaching the campuses—both high school and college. And it's definitely ministering to the youth of the establishment churches."[6]

More traditional expressions of Christianity were also affected by unique features of the Jesus Movement. Christian coffeehouses developed around the country as the Jesus Movement spread. "At the beginning," Jorstad observed, "each [coffeehouse] leader would generally follow the same pattern: rent a store in the inner city; turn it into a counseling center and coffeehouse with free sandwiches, coffee, and Kool Aid; and invite anyone interested to come in."[7]

Arthur Blessitt founded His Place in southern California, which ministered primarily to drug users, runaways, and similar individuals. First Baptist Church, Lake Jackson, Texas, sponsored the Anchor, a coffeehouse ministry on the gulf coast. Hundreds of coffeehouses soon spread across the country, including the Fisherman's Net in

---

3   Duane Pederson, *Jesus People* (Ventura, CA: Regal, 1971), 34–35.
4   "Street Christians: Jesus as the Ultimate Trip," *Time*, August 3, 1970, 31.
5   Walker L. Knight, "Faddists or Disciples?," in *Jesus People Come Alive*, comp. Walker L. Knight (Wheaton, IL: Tyndale House, 1971), 103.
6   Pederson, *Jesus People*, 36, 103.
7   Erling Jorstad, *That New-Time Religion* (Minneapolis: Augsburg, 1972), 55.

Detroit, Michigan; Agape in Columbus, Ohio; and Powerhouse in Las Vegas.[8]

Evenings in the coffeehouses centered on Bible discussions, gospel rock music of some form, and in many ways, a revival meeting. These houses differed from other rescue missions because they sought to reach young street people especially and because of their lack of ties with other churches or agencies. Many coffeehouses eventually became churches.

Ed Plowman reported on the Jesus Movement and asked those involved to explain it. A mustached young man in Washington DC told him, "It's simple: we have discovered that we can experience what you preachers have only been talking about for years."[9]

Some Jesus People began to live together in houses. Such communes had colorful names like Solid Rock House and Rejoice Always. They were generally characterized by a minimum of organization and high standards of morality and discipline.

Marches for Jesus, not unlike civil rights and other marches, began occurring around the nation. McFadden cited one march in New Orleans where "young longhairs with trumpets and drums have paraded up and down Bourbon Street imitating the traditional funeral procession in a demonstration of their faith."[10] In Fort Worth, Texas, more than 13,500 youth marched down Main Street as a part of the Texas Baptist Youth Evangelism Conference, carrying signs that said things like "Turn On to Jesus," "Jesus Is Real." The chief of police in Fort Worth called it "one of the best things he'd seen in years, 'As American as ham and eggs.'"[11]

Festivals—large gatherings of people with music, testimonies, and speakers—emerged at about the same time as Woodstock. During the

---

8   Larry R. Jerden, "Surf and Soul," *Baptist Standard*, August 13, 1969, 12–13; Michael McFadden, *The Jesus Revolution* (New York: Harper and Row, 1972), 14; and Edward E. Plowman, *The Jesus Movement in America* (Elgin, IL: Cook, 1971), 58.

9   Edward E. Plowman, *The Jesus People* (Elgin, IL: Cook, 1971), 24.

10 McFadden, *Jesus Revolution*, 11.

11 Toby Druin, "Echoes of the Movement," *Home Missions*, June–July 1971, 46.

early years of the festivals and coffeehouses, CCM as a genre appeared. Jesus rock concerts developed as the movement progressed. The first big festival was the Faith Festival in Evansville, Indiana, March 27–28, 1970. Pat Boone and several folk-rock Christian groups were the featured leaders of the festival, and the musical *Tell It Like It Is* was presented by the Indianapolis Youth for Christ musical troupe. In 1971 a Faithfest drew fifteen thousand, and on March 9, 1971, the first of a series of rallies in Chicago drew nine thousand. The state Baptist Student Union Convention in Arkansas hosted a Jesus festival as part of the meeting in 1972.[12]

Unique baptismal services also characterized the movement. Don Matison baptized almost fifty new converts in an irrigation ditch after an evangelistic meeting in Enslen Park, Modesto, California. Denny Flanders, who led the Jesus Movement ministry called Maranatha, was featured on the front page of the *Washington Daily News* with a photograph of a baptismal ceremony in the Lincoln Memorial Reflecting Pool. Mass baptisms were well known. The *Indiana Baptist* reported the baptism of about one thousand young people by Chuck Smith of Calvary Chapel, Costa Mesa, California. Jess Moody said the first ocean baptisms were performed by Fenton Moorehead, associate at First Baptist, West Palm Beach, where Moody was pastor.[13]

The Jesus Movement in the Evangelical Church

In terms of theology, the movement was, in general, within the framework of conservative evangelicalism, although charismatic Christianity dominated in many segments. An article in *Newsweek* emphasized the movement's theological correlation to traditional Christianity: "In truth . . . many of the evangelists who have attached

---

12   Plowman, *Jesus Movement in America,* 110–11; and "9,000 Attend Chicago Rally," *Indiana Baptist,* March 29, 1971, 8. Duane Pederson was the speaker the next month. "'Jesus Festival' Presents Him," *Arkansas Baptist Newsmagazine,* November 2, 1972, 9.

13   See Plowman, *Jesus Movement in America,* 55; "1,000 Baptized in California Ocean," *Indiana Baptist,* June 23, 1971, 6; and Jess C. Moody, audio interview on tape recording, August 13, 1990, Indianapolis.

themselves to the Jesus Movement preach the same law-and-order message to the young that [Billy] Graham directs to the kids' parents. 'I really dig Graham,' says Rich Weaver, 25. 'He's a pretty far-out guy.'"[14]

Two of the clearest examples of the Jesus Movement's relation to evangelicalism in general were the simultaneous occurrences of the Asbury Revival[15] and the rapid rise of Campus Crusade for Christ, International. In 1970 Asbury College experienced a powerful revival that not only affected the college there but also spread to many other campuses. Campus Crusade rode the impetus of the Jesus Movement with its Explo '72 event in Dallas, Texas. More than eighty thousand young people attended the weeklong training sessions, which focused on winning the world to Christ within a generation. The Saturday following the event a day-long Christian music festival drew crowds estimated at 150,000 to 180,000. Billy Graham, one of the speakers at Explo, called it a Christian Woodstock.

Any historic movement, particularly one where God's hand has been at work, provides a laboratory for the contemporary church to discover how biblical principles are worked out in the context of a given cultural setting. The Jesus Movement offers principles that stand beyond the "One Way" signs, psychedelic T-shirts, and coffeehouses. What, then, can the Jesus Movement contribute to contemporary youth ministry?

The Jesus Movement was just that—a movement about Jesus. It began neither as a result of strategic planning by a think tank nor as a result of human effort. In today's youth ministry, obsessed with discovery of new trends, methods, and strategies, we'd be well advised to recall that many of the most effective methods and strategies to reach the world—whether it be missions, evangelism, or specifically church growth—have been born from times of awakening.[16] The latest

---

14   "The Jesus People," 97.
15   For a concise account of the Asbury Revival, see Robert E. Coleman, ed., *One Divine Moment* (Old Tappan, NJ: Revell, 1970).
16   See Malcolm McDow and Alvin L. Reid, *Firefall: How God Shaped History Through Revivals* (Enumclaw, WA: Pleasant Word, 2002), for many examples of church growth coming from awakenings.

technology and research may be of some help but, when it comes to youth ministry, God must be the source of anything eternal. In times of mighty revival, God simply pours out his Spirit on our land and, as in the Jesus Movement, young people joined God's work.

The Jesus Movement's Effect on Church Life

In a retrospective, Walker Knight noted the rise of "super churches" following the Jesus Movement: "Twenty years ago only two or three congregations numbered near the 10,000-member mark. Today many cities can point to one or more super churches."[17]

Calvary Chapel in Costa Mesa, California, in the minds of many the mother church of the Jesus Movement, continues to be an example of the megachurch phenomenon. Beginning in 1965 with only twenty-five people, the church now has multiple thousands in attendance every week and still practices mass baptisms in the ocean.

Calvary Chapel can be said to have produced offspring as well. Numerous congregations across America began with pastors who converted to Christianity at Calvary Chapel. Scores of young men in the Jesus Movement who attended Calvary Chapel and entered the ministry now lead large churches.

One of the most recognized examples is the Horizon Christian Fellowship in San Diego. Horizon began with twelve people, and now has 6,500 worshipers each Sunday, making it one of the largest churches in California. In addition, Horizon has started more than thirty other churches. The church was founded by Mike MacIntosh, who in the late 1960s was a drug addict. He once turned himself in to the police as the "fifth Beatle." One night in 1970, MacIntosh attended Calvary Chapel. Chuck Girard and his group, Love Song, sang that night, followed by a message from Lonnie Frisbee, one of the earliest leaders of the Jesus Movement. MacIntosh committed his life to Jesus Christ, and in 1971—after moving into the communal

---

17   Walker A. Knight, "Prelude to a Spiritual Awakening," *Missions USA*, March–April 1982, 21.

house, Mansion Messiah—he and his former wife were remarried.[18] Of particular interest, before founding Horizon, MacIntosh was director of Maranatha Music, a CCM company beginning out of Calvary Chapel.

Greg Laurie, another Calvary Chapel alumnus, has become one of the better-known evangelists of the present day. Laurie also pastors Harvest Christian Fellowship in Riverside, California, with well over twelve thousand members. Converted at Calvary Chapel, Laurie began Harvest Fellowship in 1972 as a Bible study, and now speaks at Billy Graham-sized crusades. A 1991 citywide meeting in Anaheim had a total of 200,000 in attendance. At the final service 51,000 attended, the largest crowd in that stadium for such a meeting since Graham had been there ten years prior.[19]

Many Southern Baptist churches, too, became megachurches in the early 1970s. Houston's First Baptist exploded following the arrival of Pastor John Bisagno, who was both aware of and open to the Jesus Movement. During the same period, Rehoboth Baptist Church was one of Georgia's fastest-growing. Knight observed, "Such super churches as Rehoboth appear to be a legacy of the Jesus Movement and its influence."[20]

The Church Growth Movement and Youth Ministry

Following the Jesus Movement, youth leaders increasingly focused upon how to gather larger numbers of students into their ministries. Youth groups became segregated from the rest of their congregations, conducting their own worship services and events largely independent of their churches. They in essence became parachurch movements within their congregations. Students would come to the church campus and quickly separate from their parents to participate in youth Sunday school, youth worship, or youth discipleship groups.

---

18 "Memories of the Jesus Movement," 18–20. For an analysis of the ministry of Horizon see Towns, *Ten of Today's Most Innovative Churches* (Ventura, CA: Regal, 1990), 150–62.

19 *National and International Religion Report*, September 23, 1991, 8.

20 Knight, "The Jesus Movement Revisited," 4.

Describing youth ministry during the 80s into the turn of the century, Mark Oestreicher writes:

> Youth workers clamored to develop youth-y churches-within-churches that were loosely attached to, but functionally separate (and autonomous) from, the church that housed and funded them. Revolutionary ideas about connecting with teenagers in real ways got commoditized (Youth Specialties played a leading role in this), and Youth Ministry 2.0 became program-driven. The sense was—and remains, as I contend—that if we can build the right program with the coolest youth room and hip adult leaders and lots of great stuff to attract kids, then we'll experience success.[21]

It seems that youth ministry, for some, has become a product that nonprofit and for-profit ministries peddle to the churches and to youth leaders rather than a kingdom vision to contextualize the gospel so that teenagers become Christ followers. I've been to numerous youth conferences as a volunteer youth leader, a youth pastor, and now a speaker and breakout leader. Rarely, do I see many ministries emphasizing disciple-making or evangelizing students in their breakouts or exhibits. I see a great deal of buying the latest set of games or boxed curriculum that will help youth pastors save time and entertain (at worst) or engage (at best) their students in their Bible studies and midweek services. I see many products focused on helping youth ministers cut corners as they prepare to teach their lessons or lead their ministries. All of these products come with a price or a subscription. Let's face it, commoditizing youth ministry is big business and can help former youth pastors who are entrepreneurial make a fairly nice income.

So where has this stage in youth ministry gotten us? How healthy are our youth groups and the graduates who leave our ministries to start their freshman year in colleges around the country? As I men-

---

21 Oestreicher, *Youth Ministry*, 58–59.

tioned in earlier chapters of this book, the majority of our students are leaving our youth ministries and churches after they graduate. They are not transferring to other churches. They are leaving the church. In addition, we are not engaging teenagers in our communities with the gospel. Across denominational lines, churches are declining.

In spite of the decline in our churches, there are some developments in youth ministry that give me hope. Since the turn of the century we've witnessed a renewed emphasis upon the role of parents and guardians in the life of teenagers. Many youth pastors and church leaders now realize that they only have a few hours a week with students, while their parents and legal guardians are with them around the clock. This realization led to a renewed emphasis of the role of parents and guardians in youth ministry. More youth ministers and youth ministries seek to engage parents and to equip them in discipling their students. This focus upon families and parents helps to encourage a more biblical and sustainable approach to youth ministry. It also grants more potential that students will graduate with a better spiritual foundation, one partly established by their parents/guardians, as they venture into college and careers.

In addition, more youth pastors and leaders understand the importance of adult leaders in their youth ministries. Youth pastors are moving away from the model of hip charismatic youth pastor that focuses more on a personality than a healthy ministry. More and more, they are adopting an approach that emphasizes adult leaders using their spiritual gifts as they come alongside youth pastors to minister to students. Youth pastors are increasingly sharing their ministries because they understand that it is a more healthy and biblical approach. In addition, youth pastors are beginning to see how to help their students understand their connection to their local church and how the youth ministry relates to the rest of the congregation.

The focus, in the last decade, on a missional approach to our communities is also a bright spot in church life and youth ministry. More youth ministries see their communities as mission fields. They see other churches as partners rather than competitors in ministry.

Increasingly, church leaders have more of a kingdom vision rather than a myopic view of how their congregations relate to the community, the region, the country, and the world. Youth pastors and leaders are modeling this missional mindset for their students. Students are starting to see their families, friends, and schools through missional lenses.

While we have much work to do in order to raise the bar, I'm encouraged by these bright spots in youth ministry. I believe that they point the way to our future. If we want to take youth ministry to the next level and set it upon a biblical foundation, we must focus on parents, adult leaders, the church as a whole, and having a kingdom or missional vision for our community, our country, and the nations. The next part of the book will focus on the changes necessary to raise the bar.

PART 2

REINVENTING YOUTH MINISTRY

The definition of insanity is doing the same thing the same way every time and expecting different results. Part I of this book raises some serious challenges to youth ministry. We need different solutions to engage these challenges. The status quo will not solve them. Youth ministry needs to change.

In this part of the book, we'll explore changes we need to make to raise the bar in youth ministry. We need to involve parents, youth pastors, and youth leaders in developing orthodoxy (right belief), orthopathy (right affections), and orthopraxy (right practice) in the lives of teenagers. We must help students obtain a healthy understanding of worship and how we can create idols in our lives that distract us from true worship. Our parents must have a healthy understanding of the key role they play in the spiritual development of their students. Pastors and churches must understand that engaging the next generation will take teamwork on behalf of the entire staff of the church. Parents, youth pastors, and adults need to help students navigate the rites of passage and changes that occur during their development in such a way that honors God and helps them become more like Christ.

It's time to draw a line in the sand. It's time to raise the bar and kick it up a notch in youth ministry. It's time for parents, youth pastors, and youth leaders to engage the next generation with the gospel and the truth of God's Word, utilizing good old-fashioned first-century disciple-making. Are you ready to dive in? Let's go!

7

TEACHING THE YOUTH WELL
BUILDING MINISTRY ON THE WORD

Give ear, O my people, to my teaching;
incline your ears to the words of my mouth!
I will open my mouth in a parable;
I will utter dark sayings from of old,
things that we have heard and known,
that our fathers have told us.
We will not hide them from their children,
but tell to the coming generation
the glorious deeds of the LORD, and his might,
and the wonders that he has done.
He established a testimony in Jacob
and appointed a law in Israel,
which he commanded our fathers
to teach to their children,
that the next generation might know them,
the children yet unborn,
and arise and tell them to their children,
so that they should set their hope in God
and not forget the works of God,
but keep his commandments;
and that they should not be like their fathers,
a stubborn and rebellious generation,
a generation whose heart was not steadfast,
whose spirit was not faithful to God.
                              —Psalm 78:1–8

While I was in seminary, I served as a youth pastor for seven years in the same church. I was naive enough to believe that I needed to dig deep with my students in the Word of God. In seminary, I was learning about biblical theology and how to interpret Scripture. I felt like I needed to pass along what I was learning about Scripture to my students in a way that they could understand. This focus on Bible study was something they asked for.

I will never forget meeting with the search team, which included three students from the youth group. In my interview they asked, "Tim, can we have more Bible studies? Can we spend more time studying the Bible? We spend forty-five minutes playing volleyball and fifteen minutes in Bible study. Is there any way that we can reverse the time and spend fifteen minutes in games and icebreakers and forty-five minutes in Bible study?" As I listened to them, I started looking for a hidden camera. Were these students really asking for in-depth Bible study?

We dove into the Scriptures. I taught students how to read passages of Scripture within their contexts. We talked about the different genres in Scripture. Our Bible studies also focused on the authors of particular books, their audiences, and their purpose for writing. The majority of the students in the youth group were eating it up. We doubled in size and had to knock out walls in the house that served as our youth house to accommodate the growth.

In the midst of this growth and the students' interest in Scripture, I had a parent approach me wanting to talk. He said, "My son thinks your Bible studies are boring. These students aren't ready to handle doctrine. You need to make the Bible studies more fun and accessible." Basically, he was asking me to increase our time playing games and to dumb down the Bible studies. He did not think our students were capable of thinking critically about the Scriptures or that they would desire to do so.

Sadly, this dad is not alone in his perception regarding the ability of students to become serious students of Scripture. Rather than discipling students and helping them to learn how to dig deep and study the Scriptures while at the same time applying them to their lives, churches focus on dumbing down the Scriptures to appeal to the least spiritually mature student in the youth group and making the process more of an information transfer rather than a lifechanging journey involving mentors. This approach results in students who are shallow in their faith. Regarding this trend, David Kinnaman writes:

> On the one hand, we find young adults who have only a superficial understanding of the faith and of the Bible. The Christianity they believe is an inch deep. On the other, we find faith communities that convey a lot of information *about* God rather than discipling young believers to live wholly and deeply in the reality *of* God. Thus the Christianity some churches pass on is a mile wide. Put the two together and you get a generation of young believers whose faith is an inch deep and a mile wide—too shallow to survive and too broad to make a difference.[1]

If we want to see a new generation that is grounded upon the Word of God and growing into mature followers of Jesus Christ, we need to help them develop orthodoxy in their lives. Orthodoxy is simply right belief, or right doctrine. It involves serious study of the Scriptures and application of the Scriptures to contemporary and everyday life issues. Developing a biblical foundation doesn't just happen. It takes hard work. Let's examine how parents and youth leaders can pursue biblical orthodoxy in the lives of students.

Every Generation Must Be Taught Anew

As a father, I'm mindful that I am the primary discipler of my children. I do not depend upon my pastor or youth pastor to teach my children right belief or right doctrine. They are not primarily responsible for my children's understanding of Scripture or their ability to study the Bible. If my children are to possess a biblical foundation upon which to build their lives—that is, orthodoxy—then it will be-

---

1   David Kinnaman, *You Lost Me* (Grand Rapids: Baker, 2011), 114–15.

cause I passed it on to them. Every generation has a fresh opportunity to make an impact, but there's a real chance that every generation will miss the lessons from the past.

In 2 Chronicles 34 we see the account of young King Josiah and his reforms. At age sixteen Josiah began to seek the Lord, and by age twenty he was leading a major reform. The key to the change for his generation was not innovation or technology. The key was the discovery of the Law. Read the account and just imagine: God's people had lost the Bible.

I am afraid the Bible has been lost, too, in many families and youth ministries, and the result is too many Josiahs miss the chance to do great things for God. Today's levels of biblical illiteracy among students, their families, and their youth group members are skyrocketing. Regarding the number of parents who have in-depth conversations involving the Scriptures and how they relate to hard topics, the Barna Group reports, "Surprisingly, one in five says they do not feel prepared to address 'tough' questions about Christianity, God or the Bible."[2] It seems that many parents feel like they are ill equipped to teach Scripture to their students. At the same time, youth ministers are tempted to substitute innovation, technology, and shallow curriculum for biblical teaching and discipleship. As a contemporary church planter and someone who speaks regularly to students, I am all for innovation and harnessing technology; however, I would argue that the hope for the future of youth ministry must be based in *truth,* not *technique.* Before consulting the latest youth website or magazine, a good place for a youth pastor to start in raising the bar of Bible knowledge would be to read the entire Bible with an eye to its references to youth.

What can be more important to give a young person than the truth of God's Word? And this truth must be communicated in a context that encourages long-term growth and maturation, that is, in the *church.* Such an approach involves parents, youth ministers,

---

2 Barna Group, *Gen Z* (Ventura: Barna Group and Impact 360 Institute, 2018), 84.

volunteer youth leaders, and peers. Richard R. Dunn makes the point well:

> A mature theological framework considers the implications of God's design of the local church not only as a place where children and youth participate in an intentional, intergenerational faith community.
> Guiding the ministry into the faith community is critical. Students' spiritual growth is stunted if they are lacking in spiritual relationships with peers *and* adults. Peers may have the most immediate impact on an adolescent. Parents and adult mentors, however, have the most important long-term effect on students' lives. By God's design, students need to belong to and participate in the life of the local church.[3]

There's another reason we must teach biblical truth to young people. This generation will not buy doctrine just because the church says it's the truth. Bombarded by postmodern relativism on one side and anemic churches on the other, students today must be shown both *what* to believe and *why*. They must not only *hear* the truth; they must *experience* it. In a pluralistic culture, apologetics will have an increasingly vital role among Christian youth to help them build a strong personal faith.

Biblical Truth Matters

Greg Stier is on track when he states that "within the pages of Scripture we have everything we need to truly be successful in youth ministry."[4] Most youth pastors would agree with that statement, but our practice doesn't always match our theory. In defense of youth ministers, part of the reason they neglect strong biblical teaching is

---

3 Richard Dunn, "Putting Youth Ministry into Perspective," in *Reaching a Generation for Christ*, eds. Richard R. Dunn and Mark H. Centers III (Chicago: Moody, 1997), 31–32.

4 Greg Stier, *Outbreak: Creating a Contagious Youth Ministry through Viral Evangelism* (Chicago: Moody, 2002), 19.

that so many never learned how to study the Scriptures themselves. Too many youth ministers learn youth ministry from youth ministers who learn it from youth ministers. So the training they receive is essentially "monkey-see, monkey-do," which is great for learning practical tips but awful in terms of biblical reflection or evaluation of trends, movements, or methods. Further, many who have a seminary degree have taken few courses in Bible and none in the biblical languages. Thus few youth ministers have either the background to teach the Word or the ability to do theological reflection.

I have the privilege of teaching future youth pastors at a university and divinity school. I teach students in the bachelors, masters, and doctoral levels of study. When my students who feel a call to youth ministry ask me what classes they should take, I tell them to take as many theology and biblical studies classes that they can. I also encourage them to pursue a Masters of Divinity in Youth Ministry. While pursuing this degree, they will enjoy classes on theology, hermeneutics, Old Testament, and New Testament. It is a comprehensive degree that grants students a broad and solid foundation for preaching, teaching, and ministry.

There's a place for specialization, whether in education, music, youth, women's studies, or other areas, but not at the expense of significant biblical teaching. Think about it: a youth pastor teaches believers at a time when they are the most teachable and malleable. Those teaching youth should be the *most* skilled at teaching the Word, the best trained in theology, the biblical languages, and philosophy. Youth pastors are just that: pastors. They must have the equipping and ability to handle the Scriptures equal to senior pastors. I would argue that they must be equipped even more than senior pastors because they have to take the deep doctrines of Scripture and communicate them in such a way that they are accessible to middle and high school students in various developmental stages. They must also equip parents to develop skills to interpret the Scriptures and disciple their children.

Truth that is neglected by one generation is rejected by the next.

A post-Christian culture awash in a sea of relativism needs truth to be proclaimed more, not less, clearly by parents and youth leaders.

Only 4 percent of Generation Z have a biblical worldview.[5] More than any time in the history of our nation, students need to hear the Word of God.

Students require youth pastors and parents who will feed them the Word of God. They need leaders and mentors who will help them learn how to feed themselves Scripture through individual Bible study. Youth pastors and parents must teach students the core doctrines of the gospel and how to defend them, if they seek to grant a biblical foundation to the next generation. Teenagers need biblical meat, not marshmallow fluff. If you are a youth pastor who thinks that simply downloading a lesson or cramming thirty minutes before a Bible study is sufficient biblical teaching and equipping for this generation, leave youth ministry—you're causing more harm than good.

If we are to teach students the truths of the faith, we must do more than give them an anemic view of the body of Christ. We must teach in a way that helps them see the reality of Jesus every moment of every day, which includes both the imparting of truth (orthodoxy), the affections (orthopathy), and applying truth to what we do (orthopraxy).

The Gospel Still Speaks

In practice, too many youth leaders portray a subtle skepticism about the power of the Word of God to change lives. I'm still shocked that I continue to receive invitations from youth pastors to preach to their students. I'm convicted that I have nothing to offer students to whom I preach but the hope of the gospel and the truth of the Scriptures. I don't share a lot of stories. I'm definitely not trendy or cool in their eyes. I am simply a messenger who God has tasked to carry a message to parents, adult leaders, and teenagers who desperately need to hear it—the message of the gospel. Here's what I'm surprised (and convicted that I'm surprised) to see: the simple message of the gospel and the Word of God preached still change people's lives to God's glory and the advancement of his kingdom.

---

5   Barna, *Gen Z*, 13.

It seems there is an unwritten rule today that states that effective youth communicators must depend upon humor in lieu of the Bible. Many seem to believe that communicating to students and biblical exposition are mutually exclusive. Some even believe that preaching must be replaced by or propped up with drama or technology. Now I love drama and technology, yet Christian *chic* need not replace Christian truth. What students need is not the latest quote from a celebrity on Twitter or some movie that just came out; they need the unsearchable riches of God.

Now understand that most of the time the word *preach* is used in the New Testament, it simply referred to a verbal witness of the gospel—someone speaking the gospel to someone else. We need parents, youth pastors, adult volunteers, and peers who will speak and teach the gospel and the Scriptures to students. We must be serious students of the Word who mentor teenagers to become serious students of the Word if we are going to pass a biblical foundation to the next generation. The Bible and the gospel are sufficient to engage any doubt, question, or trend that surfaces in the culture in which our youth live. Youth pastors and parents must be familiar with philosophies and issues confronting our students. In addition, we must help our students apply biblical truth to everyday life and everyday questions. (Hint: you can't do this without youth pastors and parents who know God's Word.)

It's time, then, to stop giving our children a heritage of biblical illiteracy. Parents, youth pastors, and volunteer youth leaders should teach youth that biblical truth has nothing to fear. We should take on their hardest questions and doubts. It will take a team of parents, youth pastors, and adult leaders who are serious students of the Bible and diligent disciplers of teenagers to help build a biblical foundation for the members of Generation Z.

And if teaching the Bible also includes preaching the Bible, so be it. Youth do not hate preaching—they hate *boring* preaching. So do I. They can't stand services devoid of life and passion. Neither can I. They need to see how truth connects to the real world and be *challenged* to live that truth. We don't need to preach less; we need to apply more. We don't need an attractional model of youth ministry. We need a model that focuses on parents, youth pastors, and youth leaders making disciples of students—teaching, preaching, and demonstrating the Scriptures.

Barna observes:

> I am convinced that we sometimes blur the distinction between what we have to do to attract teens to the church (i.e., marketing) and what we must do to impact them for Christ (i.e., ministry). Too often, it seems, we surrender ministry value for marketing impact—that is, we give up the responsibility to facilitate life change in order to succeed at attracting a crowd.
>
> How do we do this? By performing music, dramas and offering amusing teaching rather than engaging them in authentic worship and serious discipleship. By striving to facilitate relationships rather than providing them with accountability. . . .
>
> We have mastered the art of drawing a crowd, but at the expense of drilling deep into the lives of teenagers with spiritual truths. Games, loud music, interactive discussions, silly skits—all of those means have a place in youth ministry, but they must have a meaningful connection to the ultimate purpose of the ministry. If those approaches are justified solely because they help us to recruit a larger number of young people, then we will win the battle but lose the war.[6]

What about Small Groups?

Over the past several years, Sunday school in most churches has become the dead zone. Even after a whole weekend of youth meetings in which God moves and students get excited, they can walk into

---

6 George Barna, *Real Teens: A Contemporary Snapshot of Youth Culture* (Ventura, CA: Regal, 2001), 155–56.

Sunday school and become zombies. In other small groups, teachers aren't prepared to teach or facilitate discussion about a passage. What's happened to the excitement in the church about studying God's Word?

Recall that in past great awakenings a hunger for the Word was evident. John Wesley, for example, came to Christ at a small-group meeting in which the prologue to Luther's commentary on Romans was being read—not exactly the hottest youth communication package. Yet he met Christ, and God used him to rock England for Jesus. In the First Great Awakening in the American colonies, some people began to read the Scripture, commentaries, and sermons to one another. The hunger for the Word of God grew until "reading houses" were built to accommodate the numbers of people hungering for God's Word. That desire is evident, too, in Scripture. In Ezra's day the people stood half a day as the Word was read and explained. Shouldn't our Sunday school and small group teaching, then, undergo a reformation as well? Do we really believe that the gospel and the Word of God carry life-changing power in the lives of students?

Tips for Teachers

The following provides some practical insights for those who work with youth in Sunday school and small groups.

1. Teach the Bible, not your opinion of it. Do not sit in a circle and ask, "What does this passage say to you?" Ask what *God* is saying and then apply it to the students' lives. Teaching the Bible is not the pooling of ignorance but the imparting of truth. Spurgeon is known for saying that the Bible is like a lion—you don't have to defend it, just turn it loose.

2. Remember, knowledge without application leads to frustration. Every time I prepare my messages and study for my sermons, I do it thinking about the question, "So what?" I can exegete a text and exposit its meaning to a group of students, but if I do not show them how the text applies to their everyday lives, I've not really taught or preached a passage. Especially in this post-Christian nation, people want to know what difference the Word of God and a relationship with Jesus Christ makes in their lives. Do not misunderstand: the Word of God is truth, and always relates to real life. But if people don't make that connection, they miss the very truth they need so badly.

Unless teenagers are provided with a very different spin on truth—one that is comprehensible, relevant, compelling, practical, and consistently modeled—they can be expected to follow the path of least resistance—which is the path of relativism.[7]

This connection is what is known as "experience-based learning." Teachers must avoid the usual watered-down, emotional approach to teaching, and instead help students take the truth that is placed in their heads, move it to their hearts, and help them see how it changes their lives in the real world.

3. Atmosphere matters. Andy Stanley and Stuart Hall note the importance of both the *context* and the *content* of youth ministry. They also note that most youth ministers work harder on the former than on the latter, spending much time on designing T-shirts and planning activities and less time "determining what our students need to know before finishing high school."[8] While the emphasis on context over content is especially true when it comes to Wednesday nights, I wonder if both are given enough attention for Sunday morning Bible study.

Imagine these scenes:

- *Scene 1:* You enter the classroom on Sunday morning. You're not prepared, you stayed up too late the night before, you didn't really like the lesson anyway, and your class attendance is down. You start by telling the class you're tired, ill-prepared, and disappointed in them because they haven't brought any friends. The only enthusiasm you have is for the NFL game later, and you tell them.

- *Scene 2:* On Sunday morning you rise early to spend a little extra time in prayer for each student in your class. "I wonder if John will come today?" you ask yourself, praying that to-

---

7   Barna, *Real Teens*, 94.
8   Andy Stanley and Stuart Hall, *The Seven Checkpoints* (West Monroe, LA: Howard, 2001), 4.

day John would come and meet Jesus. Having gone over the lesson, you ask God to let its truth penetrate your life. God gives you a glimpse of insight that excites you. You enter the classroom prayed up, fired up, and ready to challenge your students to be a little more like Jesus.

Do you think the two scenes above will affect the class differently? Of course they will! Each week, early in the week, ask God to make the lesson come alive for you. Seek a way for the lesson to help you better serve the Lord. Such earnest endeavor will spill over to your class. Other practical features add to atmosphere as well:

- Make the room as comfortable as possible.
- Get started on time.
- Be enthusiastic—it's contagious!
- Avoid embarrassing students—do not call on students to read the Bible or to pray publicly if they are easily embarrassed. Avoid other ways that unnecessarily single out people.
- Don't ask questions that have only a single correct answer. Try asking questions for which there are no wrong answers. For example, instead of asking, "Who was known as the encourager, and even had his name changed to that in the Bible?" Ask instead, "Can you name someone who has encouraged you? Tell me why or how?" *Then* introduce Barnabas as a biblical example. Such an approach encourages rather than discourages discussion.

4. The secret to great teaching is contagion. "What you do screams so loud I cannot hear what you say," as Emerson is said to have stated. "They will likely feel when you have been much with God. That which is on your hearts most, is like to be most in their ears," stated Puritan pastor Richard Baxter.[9] And "that which we learn with delight we will never forget," Aristotle is said to have stated. Young people will follow

---

9   Richard Baxter, "The Reformed Pastor," in *The Practical Works of Richard Baxter*, vol. 4 (London: Henry G. Bohn, 1854), 425.

your example more than your teaching. If you are excited about the things of God, they'll eventually catch your passion.

5. *See where your students could be, not where they are now.* A great teacher sees the potential in students that they don't see in themselves. A missionary was once asked how he got so many young people—who on the surface had little potential—to do great things for God. His reply was, "I put a big crown over their head and help them grow into it." That's a teacher's calling.

6. *Illustrate to educate.* A great way to teach is by analogy. The Bible is full of stories, and youth love them.

7. *Love your students.* I probably have less in common with young people than most who read this book. I'm a middle-aged professor. I live in the world of the academy. When I speak to students, I don't have automatic rapport with them. Many youth ministers seek out the "hot" speaker of the moment, adding to the insecurity of so many who teach the Bible to adults, confirming their fears that they can't communicate to youth. Paul was not the hottest thing going when he came to town. But he had the hand of God and a passion for those to whom he spoke.

If you teach adults and don't have immediate rapport with students, it's not a big deal. Be real with them. Love them. Expect them to develop a love for God's Word.

Is it true that the closer in age to youth the speaker is the better he can communicate with them? No, communicating truth is not affected by age, but it can be helped by maturity.

8. *Start well and end well.* Start your class with excitement. You have one hour a week to pour the Word of God into a group of young people, and it is an awesome honor. Because I don't have immediate rapport with students, I work very hard to get their attention in the first five minutes. I may use a question, an illustration, or an object lesson. I like to use self-deprecating humor. Remember, be yourself.

An old rule of thumb for teaching still applies: when you teach, tell them what you're going to tell them (give the point in a nutshell). Then tell them (teach the lesson). Then, tell them what you told them (summarize and apply). Creative repetition is a powerful way to teach.

End well. I try to finish every message or lesson with a specific point of application. Do not just teach about witnessing; point every student to a gospel app and challenge him or her to share it with someone. Don't just teach on forgiveness; ask students to write the name of someone they find it hard to forgive, and suggest ways to pray about forgiveness over the next week.

Here's one example. Let's say you're teaching a lesson at Christmastime. Challenge the students to turn one conversation during the next week from the secular—Santa, gifts, shopping—to the sacred—how God gave us Jesus. Remember, you, too, must do what you challenge them to do.

Setting the Bar

Finally, parents and youth leaders need to ask: What do I want my student(s) to know about the Word of God by the time they graduate and leave home? What doctrines do I want them to understand? What biblical truths should they comprehend? In response to those questions, we must develop plans to teach our students these essential truths of the faith. We need to not only teach them but also give them tools that they can use in their personal Bible study. Jesus was intentional in teaching the disciples. He knew what he wanted them to understand prior to ascending into heaven. We too must be intentional regarding what we want our students to know prior to graduation.

While they are in middle school, high school, and into college, it is not enough that students adopt the doctrines their parents, legal guardians, or youth leaders believe. They must have a solid foundation of biblical truth upon which they can stand as they seek to be salt and light to their friends in a culture that is opposed to the concept of exclusive truth. Students need to own their faith and understand from Scripture why they believe what they believe.

Such a robust faith is not built by parents and youth pastors focusing primarily on methods and methodology. It is also not accomplished by concentrating more on mediums of communication. No, we build such a foundation on biblical truth when we focus on the message we communicate.

I don't want to sound like a naysayer or a critic from the ivory towers. I don't know any youth pastors or Christian parents who have a goal of raising up a generation of spiritually anemic students. But what if parents and youth pastors decided to set a new standard, where the youth ministry was built on biblical teaching and everything else revolved around it? Games could still be played and fellowship encouraged, while biblical Christians are being grown. What if parents, youth pastors, and youth leaders developed a chart of doctrines that coincided with each grade in middle school and high school that they wanted students in that age bracket to grasp prior to leaving that grade or graduating? What if we focused our teaching as parents and youth leaders on these doctrines as our students grow up in the youth group? I think such an approach establishes a firm foundation upon which students can stand, one that relates biblical truth to what they are encountering in their everyday lives.

Resource

It's often hard to know where to start when seeking resources for teaching students Scripture. There is no curriculum that is a "silver bullet" for biblical teaching; however, it is helpful for others to suggest resources that they have used to help teach the Scriptures. The primary resource that I've found helpful for teaching basic biblical interpretation to students and adults is a book written by my two friends Matt Rogers and Donny Mathis, *Seven Arrows: Aiming Biblical Readers in the Right Direction*.[10] This book helps grant students and adults basic skills for reading and interpreting Scripture. Matt and his wife Sarah also wrote a fifty-two-week devotional study for teens based upon the approach in the *Seven Arrows*.[11]

Rogers and Mathis suggest reading the Scriptures with seven questions in mind:

---

10 Matt Rogers and Donny Mathis, *Seven Arrows: Aiming Bible Readers in the Right Direction* (Spring Hill, TN: Rainer, 2017).

11 Matt and Sarah Rogers, *Seven Arrows: A 52-Week Devotional for Teens* (Nashville: Lifeway, 2017).

1. What does this passage say?
2. What does this passage mean to its original audience?
3. What does this passage tell us about God?
4. What does this passage tell us about man?
5. What does this passage demand of me?
6. How does this passage change the way I relate to people?
7. How does this text prompt me to pray?[12]

I use *Seven Arrows* in the multiethnic church plant that I pastor. Our life group leaders use the seven questions to guide their members through the focal passage they are studying. We also encourage life group members to use the seven questions in their personal daily Bible study. The book is very helpful for establishing a baseline for helping people read and interpret Scripture. I highly recommend it as a resource for parents and youth leaders who seek to teach students the Scriptures and give them tools for studying the Bible.

We need parents and youth pastors who are committed to teaching the next generation the Word of God. In addition, students need us to show them how God's Word applies to their lives. Confluence refers to a point where two rivers join to become one. How excited young Timothy must have been to see his model Paul share how the truth was working in his life.

What's the best way, then, to impart biblical knowledge to Generation Z? If we teach with love, if we teach biblical truth and model that truth, we will teach our children well.

---

12 Rogers and Mathis, *Seven Arrows*, 20–23.

8

HABITUAL LOVE
STIRRING THE AFFECTIONS OF YOUTH

Therefore, my beloved, as you have always obeyed, so now, not only as in my presence but much more in my absence, work out your own salvation with fear and trembling, for it is God who works in you both to will and to work for his good pleasure.

—Philippians 2:12–13

And let us consider how to stir up one another to love and good works, not neglecting to meet together, as is the habit of some, but encouraging one another, and all the more as you see the Day drawing near.

—Hebrews 10:24–25

In 2001, shortly after September 11, my Kentucky Army National Guard unit deployed on Operation Noble Eagle, the homeland defense mission the military conducted to protect the continental United States against threats from al-Qaeda. A few months after we deployed, our orders were changed to Operation Enduring Freedom, the mission overseas to counter al-Qaeda. Our mission was in Europe.

Because of the deployment, I spent almost a full year away from my wife Angela and sons Micah and Noah. People often ask me how my wife and I handled being separated for such a long period of time. We did not yet have Skype, FaceTime, or any other means of using a webcam to talk over the internet, so we communicated through emails and phone calls.

Even though we were thousands of miles apart from each other, we grew in our love and affection for each other by writing to each other, reading each other's emails, and listening and talking to each other. The emails and phone conversations allowed us to share what we were experiencing and allowed opportunities for us to share our love for each other. Through these means of communication, we shared our joys, sorrows, fears, hopes, significant events, and more. While we were apart geographically, we did not miss out on things that were happening in each other's lives.

When I think of my relationship with the Lord, I think of my deployment.

Stirring Up Our Affections (Orthopathy)

We do not physically see Jesus. He ascended into heaven and left his Holy Spirit to indwell us and work in us to make us more like him. The Holy Spirit works in us the will to do God's will. He stirs our hearts to love Jesus more each day that we walk with him. This process does not occur simply by the work of the Holy Spirit. He uses what are often called spiritual disciplines to grow our affection or love for Christ.

When we speak of the affections, we are referring to orthopathy (right affections, right feelings, or the right heart). We discussed in the last chapter the importance of our students having right beliefs or doctrinal convictions—orthodoxy. It is important as well that teenagers develop the right love, heart, or affections toward God—orthopathy.

How do Christ followers, whether young or old, grow in their love for Jesus? This is an important question, as our affections, or what we love, drive our actions.

When we give our lives to Christ, the Holy Spirit indwells us. He begins the work of sanctification, making us more like Jesus. The apostle Paul wrote of the Spirit in his letter to the church in Philippi, "I am sure of this, that he who began a good work in you will bring it to completion at the day of Jesus Christ" (Phil. 1:6). The Holy Spirit stirs within us a desire to grow closer to God and to love him more. We begin to desire to read God's Word. Prayer becomes something we start thinking about, talking with, and listening to God. We want to gather with other believers in worship, Bible study, and fellowship. All of these desires are evidence of the Holy Spirit's work in our lives.

The Holy Spirit uses spiritual habits in our lives to help us grow more like Jesus. The Puritans called them means of grace. Some Christ followers call these habits spiritual disciplines. They are called disciplines because they are something that Christ followers have to do in response to the work of the Holy Spirit in our lives. As we practice these disciplines, God stirs within our hearts more love toward him. They are means through which the Spirit blows through our lives. Regarding the relationship between the spiritual disciplines and the Holy Spirit, Amy Carmichael wrote, "We have not to make the Wind or to beseech it to blow. We have nothing to do with the wonder of it. Our one work is to set our sails to catch the least whisper of it. 'Blow, blow O Breath' really only means, 'O Breath, my sails are set; according to the promise of my Lord, fill them now.'"[1]

How are we helping our students develop disciplines and habits so they can "raise the sail" to catch the Holy Spirit blowing through? What habits or disciplines do we desire they possess in middle school and high school? What are we doing to help stir the affections in our students?

In order to help answer some of these questions, let's look at some critical spiritual habits or disciplines every student needs to help him/her develop more love toward Christ and other people. The following discussion does not exhaust every spiritual discipline but begins the conversation and perhaps spurs your mind to determine what disciplines you want your students to exercise.

Reading God's Love Letter

Just like reading her emails grew my love for Angela though we were separated, we grow closer and more in love with Jesus when we

---

1   Amy Carmichael, *Candles in the Dark* (Fort Washington, PA: CLC Publications, 2017), 49.

read his love letter to us. The Holy Spirit teaches us through the Word of God. Regarding the role of the Spirit as a teacher, Jesus said, "But the Helper, the Holy Spirit, whom the Father will send in my name, he will teach you all things and bring to your remembrance all that I have said to you" (John 14:26). God the Holy Spirit is the author of Scripture (2 Tim. 3:16–17). He will illuminate God's Word as we read it and help us (and our students) to apply the truths of Scripture to our lives. The Holy Spirit teaches us who God is as we read his Word; therefore, it's imperative that students and every other Christ follower read the Word of God if they are to develop the heart that God wants them to have toward him and toward their neighbors.

In the book *Spiritual Disciplines for the Christian Life*, Donald S. Whitney puts it this way:

> No Spiritual Discipline is more important than the intake of God's Word. Nothing can substitute for it. There simply is no healthy Christian life apart from a diet of the milk and meat of Scripture. The reasons for this are obvious. In the Bible God tells us about himself, and especially about Jesus Christ, the incarnation of God. . . . We find in Scripture how to live in a way that is pleasing to God as well as best and most fulfilling for ourselves. None of this eternally essential information can be found anywhere else except the Bible. Therefore if we would know God and be Godly, we must know the Word of God—intimately.[2]

There is a plethora of resources available to help students begin the journey of developing the discipline of daily Bible reading. Numerous apps like YouVersion and One Bible are available on smartphones and portable devices. These apps offer multiple Bible reading plans that vary from small sections of Scripture each day to several chapters. There is also the option of going old school and reading a hard copy

---

2 Donald S. Whitney, *Spiritual Disciplines for the Christian Life* (Colorado Springs: NavPress, 1991), 24.

of the Scriptures. There are numerous Bible reading plans that parents, youth leaders, and students can download and print off from various internet sources. Students can read the Bible through in a year from Genesis to Revelation or use a chronological reading plan. There is no shortage of resources to help students begin this habit in their lives.

When I was a student, I was told that Jesus spent time early in the morning with the Father. Preachers at youth camp would emphasize the need for us to start the day in Scripture because that's what Jesus did. I found it very difficult as a teenager who had to leave the house at 6:45 a.m. to wake up early enough to read my Bible and get ready for school. I'd feel guilty because I just couldn't get into that pattern. Fortunately, I had a youth pastor who helped me understand that Jesus's pattern of rising early in Scripture was descriptive and not prescriptive. He emphasized that it was not so important what time of day I read Scripture, but the the main point was that I spent time daily in the Word of God. My youth pastor also gave pointers on how to develop a daily time of Bible reading. The following list includes some of those points along with ones that I've developed as a disciple and a pastor. I'm old enough now that I cannot differentiate between which ones are mine and which ones were his. They've blended together.

Here are some tips to help teens develop a time of daily Bible intake:

1. *Pick a translation that is both accurate and readable.* Help your student to choose a translation. Help them to understand the differences between translations. Stress accuracy in translation and readability. If it's not accurate, what they're reading is not the best translation. If it's not readable, they won't understand it.

2. *Choose a consistent time of the day to read the Bible.* Although I was often told as a teenager that I had to have my Bible reading time early in the morning, I found that the most productive time to read the Bible was when I was most alert and most focused. Encourage your teenager to read his/her Bible during a time of day that they are alert, focused, and not in a rush.

3. *Start with fifteen minutes of Bible reading and prayer.* Students need to start small when developing a habit of daily devotions. They can manage fifteen minutes a day. At first the goal is consistency. My experience has been that teens increase the time they spend reading God's Word as they become more consistent. The Holy Spirit gives them a hunger for the Bible the more they read it.

4. *Ask questions of the text you're reading.* As I mentioned in the previous chapter, it is important that we give students tools for biblical interpretation. As a church planter, I encourage my church members to use the questions given in the *Seven Arrows* book I mentioned previously. Whatever tool you use, help your students to interpret what they are reading.

5. *Meditate on part of the passage you are reading.* Pick a part of the passage and think about it as you go through your day. You might also memorize the section of Scripture that the Holy Spirit uses to stir you as you read. Meditating on Scripture will help students fight the spiritual battles they encounter each day. Focusing on these passages also encourages them in their daily walk.

6. *Keep a journal of your thoughts as you read Scripture.* Write down your thoughts and responses to the passage you are reading in a journal. Share how the Holy Spirit applies a particular passage to your life at that moment. Communicate your reflections regarding the meaning of the passage and what it teaches you about following Christ. Write about how it stirs your affections toward him.[3]

Although this list is not exhaustive, it includes some useful tips for helping students develop the habit of daily biblical intake. As they develop a consistent habit of reading God's Word, the Holy Spirit will stir your students' love for the Lord. They will grow closer to him as

---

3 I present these tips based on my own development in the spiritual disciplines and on my experience in discipling teenagers and adults as a pastor and youth pastor.

they read his love letter to them. Loving God more also prompts them to love people more because they see God's love for them. Daily Bible intake will also help your students mature in the faith.

Parents, youth pastors, and youth leaders, be sure as you teach students how to read God's Word that you are having a daily time of Bible intake as well. You cannot disciple them with integrity if you are not practicing the habits you are encouraging in their lives. Students need to see you model Bible intake as well as teach them how to do it. The spiritual disciplines are more caught than taught.

The Power of Prayer

Youth leader, consider this: Do those you lead see you as a person of prayer? Do they see in you a hunger to know God? Parents, do your children recognize the fruit of your daily devotional life? Are they learning from your teaching and example how to walk with God? Are you praying God-sized prayers in the ministry of your church?

Revival is a lifestyle of obedience to God, and such a lifestyle is born out of a life of prayer. I define prayer this way: *intimacy with God that leads to the fulfillment of his purposes.* Intimacy is more than just talking. Prayer paves the road to a close, daily, personal walk with our Lord, which in turn leads to the fulfillment of his purposes. Although we may pray for the needs of ourselves and others, prayer is not merely a wish list for a benefactor like Santa Claus; it is our way to learn God's purposes for us. Remember, life is not primarily about us but about him.

How do you teach youth to begin daily prayer time? Start by observing your own daily prayer time. Below are some practical tips to help you have a daily, close walk with God.

1. *Read the Bible.* As you set aside time daily, start by reading the Bible. If you don't know where to begin, try reading a chapter of Proverbs each day, reading a chapter that goes with the day of the month (Proverbs 1 for May 1, for example).
2. *Keep a spiritual journal.* I've kept one for many years. Many of the spiritual giants in history—John Wesley, David Brainerd,

George Whitefield, Jim Elliot—kept a journal. I like to write a little about the day before (I usually start out with "Yesterday I . . ."). Then I share my requests and sometimes my plans.

3. *Follow a pattern.* Jesus offered us a pattern for prayer in the model prayer found in Matthew 6. This prayer, also called the Lord's Prayer, is not a formula to repeat but a model to emulate. Notice these features that can help guide our praying:

- *God is close:* "Our Father . . ." We can know God intimately through Christ. *Begin by acknowledging the wonder of salvation* that allows us to speak to the Creator of the universe with such a personal term as "Father."

- *God is far:* "Who is in heaven . . ." God is not the "man upstairs." We can approach him intimately as Father yet with deep reverence as the great God who lives in a "high and lofty place" (Isa. 57:15). *Take time to reflect on his greatness.*

- *God is holy:* "Hallowed be your name . . ." The essential attribute of God is holiness. Throughout the Bible the threefold cry toward God is never "love, love, love" or "judge, judge, judge" but "holy, holy, holy." This reminds us of both the uniqueness of our God and the depravity of our sin. *Allow the Spirit to show you any unconfessed sin or unresolved issues, and bring them to God in confession and repentance.*

- *God is redeemer:* "Your kingdom come, your will be done . . ." How is the kingdom of God established? Through the gift of eternal life in Christ. So this prayer includes a focus on evangelism, for when we pray for the kingdom to come, we pray for all to be a part of God's family; when we pray for his will to be done, we are reminded that it is not God's will that any perish but that all come to know him (see 2 Peter 3:9). *Take time to pray for lost people, that the kingdom of God would become theirs through salvation.*

- *God is provider:* "Give us this day . . ." While the kingdom comes before other needs, God is concerned for our lives. *We can pray for the temporal, physical, and emotional needs of ourselves and others. In fact, we must!*

- *God is merciful:* "Forgive us . . ." *Here we can pray for both our sins and our willingness to forgive others.* If we daily take time to confess and forsake our sin and in that light to forgive those who hurt us, life will be much better.
- *God is our guide:* "And lead us not . . ." *Pray for direction in decisions, not toward evil, but toward him.*
- *God is worthy of praise:* "For thine . . ." *Beginning prayer time with a focus on God and ending with praise makes the time of prayer a blessing indeed.*

Another simple way to help a young believer learn to pray is by suggesting and following the guide: ACTS.

- *A is for Adoration.* Spend some time praising God for his greatness. You might listen to a praise and worship song as part of this time or read a psalm of praise like Psalm 100 or 150.
- *C is for Confession.* Ask God to reveal your sins, and then confess them (1 John 1:9). Reading the Bible sometimes helps to reveal a sin that you need to address.
- *T is for Thanksgiving.* Growing Christians are grateful Christians. Thank God for salvation and for his specific blessings.
- *S is for Supplication.* This is a big word meaning to ask God for your needs and for the needs of others. How do you know God answers if you aren't praying specifically? I like to keep a list of specific things for which I am praying. Then, when God answers, I write that down, which really encourages me.

Just as my conversations with Angela helped me grow closer to Angela, even though we were geographically separated, a daily time of talking and listening to God will help us and our students grow more in love with him.

This Generation Holds the Key

Youth are capable of discovering the basis of a revived life. Those students who are on the road of revival are there not because of wishful thinking or emotional exuberance. They're there because they've put up the sails to catch the blowing of the Holy Spirit. Their exercise of the spiritual disciplines or the means of grace in their lives stirs their affections to love God and love their neighbor more. Through the reading of the Bible, they know they've been purchased, rescued, and ransomed by a gracious God. This knowledge leads to gratitude, worship, and true inner joy. When young people choose to confess their sin and devote themselves to Christ, most of them become keenly aware of the ravages of sin in their lives and in our culture. It is against this backdrop that God seems to be moving teenagers into a new frontier.

Youth are capable, too, of knowing that God can use them mightily. As established in part 1 of this book, God has a heart for the young. Biblical history, as well as church history, reveals that when God moves in dramatic ways, young people are often at the center of the movement or are the ones most greatly affected. The traits of youthful believers should, then, give us hope—and perspective—for today and the future. Let us, then, allow God to use that passion, teaching our youth the power in a life of spiritual discipline.

At the same time, students need authentic relationships with more mature believers who encourage them and hold them accountable in pursuing spiritual disciplines. Youth have so many superficial and fake relationships on social media. Teenagers need positive personal relationships with other Christ followers who will meet with them face-to-face on a weekly basis and challenge them in their personal faith. Regarding feelings of loneliness among teens, Jean Twenge notes, "The loneliest teens are those who spend more time on social media and less time with their friends in person."[4] Christians have a powerful opportunity to show gospel community and gospel encouragement to teens in their churches and communities through personal discipleship relationships that help them to develop the spiritual disciplines in their lives.

Imagine the impact that teenagers who have their affections stirred by the Holy Spirit and the spiritual disciplines can make upon our

---

4   Jean Twenge, *iGen* (New York: Atria, 2017), 80–81.

communities and culture. What would happen if the members of the largest generation in the history of our nation displayed a growing love for God and for their neighbor? I contend that such mobilization of teenagers with their affections stirred would spark a mighty movement of God in our nation!

A Word to Parents

Many people today complain that prayer has been taken out of public schools. But how many of those who complain pray with their children in their homes?

Parents should be their children's primary encouragers in developing spiritual habits. Sadly, according to Timothy Paul Jones, "More than half of parents said that their families never or rarely engaged in any sort of family devotional time. Of the minority that did practice some sort of family devotions, one-fourth admitted that these devotional times were sporadic."[5] Regarding parents modeling prayer for their students, Jones laments, "Nearly one-fourth of parents never or rarely prayed with their children; another one-fourth only prayed with their children occasionally."[6] It's imperative that pastors and church leaders help parents to practice daily spiritual disciplines and teach them to their children. Such discipleship will obviously involve providing a model of this discipleship approach for parents to follow. In a later chapter, I'll focus specifically on what parents can do to raise the bar for their students. For now, understand that parents should be the primary disciplers of their teenagers and help them to develop spiritual disciplines in their daily lives.

The spiritual disciplines matter, and young people should learn how to communicate with God personally and read his Word while they are still children. Why? Our culture has robbed youth of their sense of wonder, of awe toward God. A way to keep a sense of wonder among youth comes through regular times of prayer and Bible reading.

---

5   Timothy Paul Jones, *Family Ministry Field Guide* (Indianapolis: Wesleyan, 2011), 27.

6   Jones, *Family Ministry Field Guide*, 28.

The church itself has abetted in the robbery. Churches argue over worship style and whether or not to clap, while neglecting the weightier matters of substance and the presence of the Spirit. We as parents and leaders of youth can raise the bar of prayer and Bible intake for this generation, starting with our own walk with God. If we teach youth the central role of prayer and Bible reading, the impact on the church could be staggering.

Greg Stier utilizes a prayer-dare-share strategy of leading youth to witness. He starts with prayer, challenging students to pray weekly for their unsaved friends by name in Sunday school or a youth meeting. Regarding the reason for this approach, Stier contends, "It only takes a cursory reading of the book of Acts to see that prayer was the engine of every move the early believers made. Their 'pray first' philosophy drove their strategy, problem solving, group meetings and disciple multiplication efforts."[7] As a professor of evangelism, I often point out that the majority of our prayer requests in churches are health-related. I encourage them to pray for their lost friends and family members. The Bible, of course, teaches us to pray for the sick. But what about praying for harvesters (Matt. 9:36–38)? What about praying for the kingdom of God to increase (Matt. 6) and remembering that it does so by the salvation of the lost? What about praying for lost friends, emulating the passion of Paul in Romans 10? We can pray for those who are sick physically, but how much more should we pray for those who are currently dead spiritually (Eph. 2)?

Such is the challenge Stier gives to youth. He adds, "I am not talking [only] about casual prayer once a week. . . . I am talking about intense, intentional prayer every day. I am talking about kids making up top ten lists of their friends and family members and praying consistently both in and out of their youth groups for the people on those lists."[8]

---

7   Greg Stier, *Gospelize* (Arvada: D2S Publishing, 2015), 73.
8   Greg Stier, *Outbreak: Creating a Contagious Youth Ministry through Viral Evangelism* (Chicago: Moody, 2002), 107.

I have the privilege of leading a multiethnic, multigenerational church plant. We pray often for people who don't know Christ. These prayers for our lost family members and friends are the power behind our growth as a church. I'm convicted that we will not share the gospel as effectively if we cease to pray for opportunities to have gospel conversations with the folks in our community. Prayer keeps our heart tender and alert to see people around us who don't know Jesus.

Youth groups and student ministries are no different than our church plant. Stier is on point in his claim, "When you inspire your teenagers to begin to pray for their unreached peers, their hearts become more and more in tune with God's."[9]

Five years from now the spiritual condition of your students will not be determined by your programs or activities. It will not be gauged by your teaching on worship. No, the number-one reason your students will be stronger spiritually five years from now is because they have learned spiritual disciplines like prayer and Bible intake. Although there are other disciplines students need to learn, these two are foundational.

---

9 Stier, *Gospelize*, 97.

9

GET REAL
SHARING JESUS CONSISTENTLY

And Jesus came and said to them, "All authority in heaven and on earth has been given to me. Go therefore and make disciples of all nations, baptizing them in the name of the Father and of the Son and of the Holy Spirit, teaching them to observe all that I have commanded you. And behold, I am with you always, to the end of the age."

—Matthew 28:18–20

But you will receive power when the Holy Spirit has come upon you, and you will be my witnesses in Jerusalem and in all Judea and Samaria, and to the end of the earth.

—Acts 1:8

I was born in Kassel, Germany, and grew up around the world. My father was an enlisted soldier in the United States Army for thirty-two years. That meant that, from the time I was born until I enrolled in college, my family moved every four or five years. While it was hard not to see extended family for years at a time, my family got to see the world. We lived in Okinawa, Japan, for four years and got to travel around that island and to other places in the Pacific. When we lived in West Berlin in the '80s, we got to see much of Europe.

In each of our duty stations overseas, we found a church family. This family did not look like most of the churches I've encountered in the United States. While in Japan, we shared a building with a Japanese congregation. The American and Japanese Christians would periodically come together to eat meals and fellowship with each other. During my teenage years, we worshiped in an international church in West Berlin. Our church members were from Germany, America, the United Kingdom, Indonesia, Vietnam, Cambodia, Lebanon, and multiple other places. As a child and a teenager, I got a glimpse into what it looks like when Christians obey the Great Commission. They get to see people from every nation come to Christ and fellowship in the unity of the gospel. Worshiping in such diverse churches helped me to develop a better understanding of the vastness of the kingdom of Christ. It brought to life Jesus's admonition, in Matthew's Gospel, to make disciples of people from *panta ta ethne*—every nation, or every ethnic group.

Sadly, when I see most youth groups, I do not see students who possess kingdom vision or what we now call a missional mindset. Most of the students I've encountered as a youth pastor and pastor do not think past their town, at worst, or past the United States, at best. In addition, I've not seen many youth groups that reflect the demographic diversity of the towns in which they are located. Before we throw shade on these students or youth groups, we must first understand that they are simply a reflection of the adults in their churches. Students will follow leadership. We cannot expect to have missional students or missional youth groups if we are not missional leaders, youth pastors, and parents who disciple students.

How do we get there? How do we help our students to develop a passion for the gospel, their communities, and the nations?

It involves the process of discipleship we've mentioned briefly in the previous two chapters. We must help students develop orthodoxy (right belief), orthopathy (right affections), and orthopraxy (right practice). Right practice does not result from getting students in a room and doing an information dump. Like orthodoxy and orthopathy, orthopraxy is also the result of discipleship.

So, what discipleship method do we use? How do we multiply student disciples like Jesus commanded? How do parents grow young men and women to become mighty witnesses who engage the darkness of the world with the light of Christ?

In the church, we are quite adept at shaking our fist at the shadowy side of society. We hurl names at the cultural darkness of our day, throwing rocks into the pit of contemporary ungodliness. But the way to remove darkness is to turn on the light. None of us as individuals can change society as a whole, but we can change *our* world. We cannot touch the life of every troubled youth, but we can influence the life of some young person. We can challenge youth to be witnesses, to live authentic lives that count for something.

This is not a day for building youth ministry on entertainment, yet that seems to be the rage. We must instead emphasize taking the zeal of youth and channeling it into adventurous and challenging opportunities like evangelism. We want students who speak the gospel with their lips and practice the gospel through their lives. We have an opportunity to affect a significant part of the youth culture through our churches. So instead of trying to out-world the world, why not challenge youth to experience the adventure of a radically changed life through Christ?

More Caught Than Taught

What is the definition of insanity? It's doing the same thing, the same way, every time, and expecting different results.

The approach to youth ministry in most churches is insane. We expect teenagers to speak the gospel and live holy lives simply from sitting in a small group and corporate worship service and receiving an information dump. I'm not taking away from the power of the Holy Spirit to change lives. I'm also not downplaying the effectiveness of the Word of God. What I am saying is that Jesus never intended the Great Commission's goal of making disciples to be achieved by an information dump. In Matthew's account, Jesus did not tell the disciples to make disciples by teaching them all that I have commanded you. He said that we make disciples by "teaching them *to observe* all that I have commanded you" (Matt. 28:20). Jesus is talking about helping people apply his teaching to their lives. He is describing an approach of teaching by example for someone else to follow. That sounds like what he did, doesn't it?

So this discipleship process involves teaching our students the Word of God and how to study the Bible. We talked about that in our chapter on orthodoxy. Making disciples also includes helping students develop spiritual disciplines or habits that stir their affections—their love for God and for their neighbors. That discussion occurred in the previous chapter on orthopathy. If we are to help students practice or apply the teachings of Jesus in their lives, we must first model them. This modeling will help students to develop orthopraxy (right practice).

Going Retro

If we're going to disciple students and lead them to make disciples, it would be wise for us to ask the question, "How did Jesus make disciples?" That's exactly the train of thought that led Robert Coleman, a giant in the area of evangelism and discipleship, to write his classic work *The Master Plan of Evangelism*.[1] While neither Coleman nor I would say that his book is the "last word" on evangelism, I believe it is a must-read for people who seek to be disciple-makers, whether they are parents, youth leaders, youth pastors, or students. Allow me to give an overview of Coleman's description of Jesus's methodology and how it relates to helping students develop right practices and share Jesus consistently.

Selection: Jesus chose the disciples. He approached the disciples and called them to follow him. Coleman discusses how Jesus chose twelve men and, among that group, poured more into three (Peter, James, John).[2] While it might seem counterintuitive, it is more effective to pour into a few students than to try to disciple multitudes. Youth pastors, youth leaders, and parents need to select a few students

---

1   Robert Coleman, *The Master Plan of Evangelism* (Grand Rapids: Revell, 1993).
2   Coleman, *Master Plan of Evangelism*, 30–31.

to lead to Christ and disciple. For parents, this choice is easy because your first disciples are your children.

Association: Jesus spent time with the disciples. They were with him every day experiencing the normal events like meals or watching him perform supernatural miracles. They learned from both. We need to spend time with our students as well. We disciple them while they experience the ordinary and extraordinary events in our lives. Spending time with them is key.

Consecration: The disciples had to set themselves aside and commit to the task of following Jesus. They were all in. At the same time, discipling students is a two-way street. Teenagers have to set aside the time and energy it takes to be discipled. They must commit to discipleship. By the way, parents, this commitment is not something you can force on them.

Impartation: Jesus gave the disciples himself. When he ascended, he sent the Holy Spirit to indwell, encourage, empower, convict, and teach them. We cannot share what we do not have. If our goal is to make disciples of our students, we must first be the disciples that God wants us to be. Then, we can impart ourselves to them, giving them Christlike models to follow.

Demonstration: Jesus showed the disciples what he wanted them to do before asking them to do it. He taught them how to pray by praying. They learned to teach and preach by watching him do it. We too must demonstrate what we want our students to do as disciples. They must see us reading the Bible, praying, sharing the gospel, and using our gifts in ministry, as well as the other aspects of our lives we want to see in theirs.

Delegation: After Jesus demonstrated what he wanted the disciples to do, he sent them out to do it. He started to do this early on in their discipleship process. We too must delegate the responsibilities of disciple-making and exercising spiritual gifts in ministry to our students. One reason why students leave the church after they graduate is because no one ever shared the ministry with them within or outside of the church. We must delegate the mission of disciple-making and the ministry of the church to our students.

Supervision: When the disciples completed what Jesus assigned them to do, they came back to him for a debrief. He would discuss what they did and give infinitely wise feedback to help them for their future efforts. We too need to supervise our disciples. When students are doing ministry or sharing the gospel, they should come back to the person discipling them for feedback and insights.

Reproduction: Jesus's expectation was that his disciples make disciples. They were to reproduce themselves. That's just what New Testament disciples did. We cannot say we've made disciples of our students if they are not also making disciples. Part of being a disciple is obedience to Jesus's command to make disciples.

Imagine the impact parents, youth pastors, and youth leaders would make if they followed this pattern of disciple-making. It will take them dying to themselves to invest in the next generation. They will need to spend their most precious commodity, time, to see students come to Christ. Students will never know what it means to observe all that Jesus commanded until they see another person living out the life of a disciple. Are you willing to put yourself in the spotlight and under the microscope to model being a Christ follower for your students? This might seem like an impossible task if left to ourselves. Let Jesus's final words in Matthew's account of the Great Commission encourage you: "And behold, I am with you always, to the end of the age" (Matt. 28:20b).

Following Our Lead

Generation Z offers the potential to become the largest number of evangelists and missionaries ever to hit the American or global culture. This generation may also produce the most zealous witnesses of any generation. And their zeal is much needed. Generation Z is the most unevangelized group of students in recent history. It's time for parents, youth pastors, youth leaders, and students who claim the name of Jesus to engage lost students. The current climate in our churches and culture reminds me of a quote from Charles Haddon Spurgeon: "Brethren, do something, do something, do something. While committees waste their time over resolutions, do something.

While societies and unions are making constitutions, let us win souls. Too often we discuss, and discuss, and discuss, and Satan laughs in his sleeve. I pray you be men of action all of you."[3]

Students will not move to action on behalf of their lost friends until they see models they can follow. They will not do evangelism in a vacuum. Someone must first demonstrate to them how to engage their peers in gospel conversations before they will initiate them with their friends. They are looking at their parents, youth pastors, and adult leaders for guidance and examples of what it looks like to be missional and evangelistic. If we want evangelistic ,missionally minded students, we must be evangelistic, missionally minded role models for them to follow. They will duplicate what we model.

So I need to ask you some hard questions: What is the name of the last person you led to Christ? When did it happen? Are you having gospel conversations with people in your community on a regular basis? Your answers to these questions relate to whether you are someone who will lead students to possess a missional mindset and share the gospel.

As a parent or youth leader you will never be neutral. You are either leading students to know Jesus better or nudging them away from him. And because the passion that youth bring to witnessing can affect a whole church, the stakes are simply too high for us to be indifferent toward modeling evangelism.

Greg Stier writes, "A handful of students in one dead church can remind the adults of what this Christianity thing is all about." I have seen this happen personally on a number of occasions. "Passionate evangelism," writes Stier, "burning in the hearts of on-fire teens can set a whole congregation ablaze."[4]

Youth develop a burden for the gospel when they see their adult leaders lead people to Christ. Dave Rahn and Terry Linhart did a

---

3   Charles Haddon Spurgeon, *Lectures to My Students* (Lynchburg, VA: Old-Time Gospel Hour, 1875), 36.

4   Greg Stier, *Outbreak: Creating a Contagious Youth Ministry through Viral Evangelism* (Chicago: Moody, 2002), 63

study of students that revealed the pivotal role adults play in modeling evangelism for their students. They found:

> When student leaders saw adults lead someone to Christ at least weekly, they reported leading more than eight friends to Christ themselves. If they observed adults evangelizing only monthly, student leaders were likely to lead fewer of their friends (four to eight) to Christ. Our research showed this to be a consistent trend. *The more often adults were observed leading others to Christ, the more often student leaders led their own friends to Christ.* When adults engaged in observable evangelistic practices less frequently, student leaders followed their pattern. The students who reported seeing adults only occasionally—if ever—evangelize were also likely to report not having led anyone to Christ.[5]

As a parent or youth leader, you can have a very positive or negative impact upon your students' stewardship of the gospel. They will only be as evangelistic as the adults they follow.

If you're a parent or youth leader who hasn't led your students in witnessing because *you* are afraid or feel unprepared, here's some advice:

1. *Be honest.* Tell your students you're learning. They want a real person, not superman.
2. *Be a learner.* Learn to share your faith. For starters, check out Greg Stier's book *Gospelize.*
3. *Be a grower.* Let them see you're willing to grow and be changed.

Take students with you as you go into the community and have gospel conversations with people. Let them see how you meet strangers and get to know them. Show them how to include the gospel in your

---

5   David Rahn and Terry Linhart, *Evangelism Remixed: Empowering Students for Courageous and Contagious Faith* (El Cajon, CA: Youth Specialties, 2009), 35.

conversations without making it a presentation. Model the listening skills you want them to have so they can get to know a person's story and where he/she is spiritually. By taking these steps, you model evangelism and encourage them to follow your example in their schools, communities, and families.

We must encourage and unleash them to do evangelism before students will share the gospel.

Mobilizing a Generation

I will never forget training with my soldiers in August of 2001 at Fort Knox, Kentucky. We sat down to eat our MREs (meals ready to eat), and the men began to talk about how they would never put their training to use in combat. I could sense that the thought that the unit would never be mobilized in defense of the country lowered morale. Some of these soldiers trained for years to defend the nation, but they never got an opportunity to mobilize or deploy.

But this is precisely how the church often treats youth. We teach them to share their faith, but do we let them deploy to engage the darkness in their families, schools, and communities? Do we take them out into the world to put their training to the test? Do we encourage them to treat the church and the youth group like an aircraft carrier rather than a luxury cruise liner? Carriers send planes out on missions. Folks on a cruise liner rarely get off the boat.

Students who have left the church after graduation say that they never felt the church gave them responsibilities or ministries to perform. They never sensed they were part of the church. They did not feel like they had a mission.

What would happen if we gave our students a vision for reaching their lost friends and family members with the gospel? What if we helped them see their families, schools, and communities as their mission field? What if we commissioned them and deployed them into the field?

Many Christian young people have the burden, but they have not been trained and encouraged to evangelize. I totally agree with the following quote by Len Taylor and Richard Ross:

> By mobilizing [students'] efforts and empowering them
> to be missionaries, they can be Great Commission Chris-
> tians, accomplishing the work of ministry. Sometimes we
> sell short the capabilities of these youths and fail to equip
> them for ministry. The church needs youth ministry built
> on new principles. Drawing a crowd is not enough. We
> have been good at drawing crowds of youth. But, if pizza
> gets them to church, what will take them out?[6]

Youth aren't interested in more pizza. They want to be challenged
with a mission that is bigger than they are. The mission with which
we must engage them is the *missio Dei* the mission of God in the
Great Commission.

Get Real about Love

Teach your youth not only to invite their lost friends but to be
patient with them. A tremendous need is evident in youth groups,
for example, to teach young women biblical modesty in their dress.
But a lost young woman need not be singled out for her attire if she
doesn't know any better. Teach guys to behave like gentlemen but to
exercise gentleness if an unruly student shows up who has no idea
how to act in church.

Douglas Hyde notes how Communists appealed to the idealism of
youth: "The Communists' appeal to idealism is direct and audacious.
They say that if you make mean little demands upon people, you will
get a mean little response which is all you deserve, but if you make
big demands on them, you will get a heroic response."[10]

Get Real about the Gospel

Youth pastors and youth leaders, while you're learning and growing, share the gospel in your youth meetings. Teach the Word, but
include the gospel in your teaching. Why? More than 80 percent of

---

6   Richard Ross and Len Taylor, *Leading and Evangelistic Youth Ministry* (Nashville: Lifeway, 1999), 59.

professions of faith occur before age twenty. And Barna found that about half of the youth who call themselves Christians and participate in youth groups in a typical month are not actually believers. That means around seven million unsaved youth are in church regularly.[7]

Charles Haddon Spurgeon, the prince of preachers, said to exegete the text, expound the Scriptures, and plow a furrow to the cross. How sad would it be for a student to bring a lost friend to the youth meeting when the speaker does not offer the gospel.

Church members, adults and youth, must be prepared to welcome lost youth. Lost youth are going to act lost because they are! One Sunday I was approached by a deacon of the church where I was serving. He came to tell me a few students were skateboarding in front of our worship center. A nearby elderly lady said, "We need to put up a sign indicating there is to be no skate boarding." Fortunately, I had a pastor who looked for a teachable moment. He began that morning worship service off with these words: "There are some young people here that we have been trying to get to come to our church for weeks. Isn't that great that they are here today?" He invited them to bring their friends the next week. He also said he would meet them after church for an exhibition of their skateboarding talents![8]

Parents and youth leaders, if you are looking for resources for sharing the gospel, there are numerous tools people can use. Some folks use the Romans Road for walking through the passages in Romans that deal with the person and work of Jesus Christ. Others use the bridge illustration that is commonly seen in the *Steps to Peace with God* material that the Billy Graham Evangelistic Association published. The 3 Circles approach is another effective way to share the gospel.[9]

Greg Stier's Dare 2 Share approach is another excellent way to involve youth in witnessing. His approach includes Prayer (praying

---

7   George Barna, *Third Millennium* (Ventura, CA: Barna Research, 1999), 59.

8   Richard Ross and Len Taylor, *Leading and Evangelistic Youth Ministry* (Nashville: Lifeway, 1999), 17.

9   You can find the 3 Circles method at www.lifeonmissionbook.com. You can also download the Life On Mission app to use the *3 Circles* approach on your smartphone or mobile device.

for lost friends), Dare (challenging lost friends to come to church to hear the gospel), and Share (unleashing youth to witness to their peers). The approach Dare 2 Share uses in witnessing follows the acrostic GOSPEL:

- God created us to be with him.
- Our sins separate us from God.
- Sins cannot be removed by good deeds.
- Paying the price for sin, Jesus died and rose again.
- Everyone who trusts in him alone has eternal life.
- Life with Jesus starts now and lasts forever.[10]

Stier, who has spent much more time than I have with youth pastors, asks of youth pastors a series of sobering questions, paraphrased below:

1. When is the last time you shared your faith?
2. Do you talk about evangelism more than you do it?
3. Are you so busy doing good things that you can't do great things (like witnessing)?
4. Are you so busy studying the latest youth fad or technology that you fail to study the Scriptures to get a word from God?
5. Do you burn with a passion to reach every lost youth in your area for Christ?[11]

That's what can happen when we show youth what it means to get real, when we model authentic witnessing. Evangelism is caught more than it is taught.

---

10 Stier, *Outbreak*, 195. You can also find this approach on Dare 2 Share's "Life in 6 Words" app.
11 Stier, *Outbreak*, 238.

10

LIFE IS WORSHIP
RECALIBRATING THE FOCUS OF STUDENTS

> Jesus answered, "The most important is, 'Hear, O Israel: The Lord our God, the Lord is one. And you shall love the Lord your God with all your heart and with all your soul and with all your mind and with all your strength.'"
>
> —Mark 12:29–30

> I appeal to you therefore, brothers, by the mercies of God, to present your bodies as a living sacrifice, holy and acceptable to God, which is your spiritual worship. Do not be conformed to this world, but be transformed by the renewal of your mind, that by testing you may discern what is the will of God, what is good and acceptable and perfect.
>
> —Romans 12:1–2

As I write this chapter, the United States just experienced a weekend unprecedented in recent history. People, in churches throughout the country, worshiped in their living rooms watching praise teams sing and pastors preach to empty seats and pews on a livestream broadcast of their worship services. The coronavirus prevented these church members from assembling together for corporate worship. They worshiped as families and individuals in their own homes. With this change in corporate worship came the concern about what folks would do without being able to assemble together.

People are asking whether worship, as we know it, will die. They wonder if, after the virus clears, people will return to their worship centers and sanctuaries to worship together with their fellow church members. These events bring worship into the spotlight. They prompt us to ask questions like: What is worship? What is the relationship between individual, family, and corporate worship?

These events point to the fact that worship is less a corporate act that can be done privately and more a private act that can be done corporately. So one's daily walk with God is critical to one's corporate worship. And corporate worship has a powerful role in the life of a believer. This role is even more powerful with youth, who thrive on meetings—such as worship services—for encouragement and edification. Corporate worship helps students sense their belonging to the church, especially if they are allowed to help lead in it.

Worship involves far more, however, than a service or music. Worship is a lifestyle, not just a one-hour meeting in a particular building. In the book of Romans, in chapters 1–11, Paul's vast theological treatise shows how biblical orthodoxy (right belief) and orthopraxy (right practice) come together in worship. Then in 12:1–2, he offers a biblical paradigm for worship. In its essence, then, worship has nothing to do with either a church building, a certain time or day of the week, or music. It has to do with offering ourselves to God with all our heart, soul, mind, and strength. It involves orthodoxy, orthopathy, and orthopraxy working together in the life of the individual.

Loving God: Heart, Soul, Mind, and Strength

Worship involves the total person. In Mark's Gospel, Jesus commands us to love God with "all your heart and with all your soul and with all your mind and with all your strength" (Mark 12:29–30). These aspects of our personhood relate the discussion in the previous three chapters about orthodoxy, orthopathy, and orthopraxy. William Hendrickson puts it this way:

> Heart, soul, mind and strength must co-operate in loving God. The *heart* is the hub of the wheel of man's existence,

the mainspring of all his thoughts, words, and deeds (Proverbs 4:23). The *soul*—the word used in the original has a variety of meanings . . . is here probably the seat of man's emotional activity; the *mind* is not only the seat of and center of his purely intellectual life but also of his dispositions and attitudes. In the Hebrew original (and also in the LXX) of Deuteronomy 6:5 the reading is "heart, soul, and might (or power)." Mark 12:30 has "heart, soul, mind, and *strength*" (cf. Luke 10:27). No essential difference is intended. We must not begin to overanalyze. What is meant in all these passages is that man should love God with all the "faculties" with which God has endowed him.[1]

Let's explore what it means for students to love God with their heart, soul, mind, and strength—and discuss how this relates to worship and orthodoxy, orthopathy, and orthopraxy!

Loving God with Our Minds
Our society is so fast-paced that we rarely take the time to just think. I see this deficit when students arrive at our university. Largely, our incoming college freshmen have not thought critically about their faith, culture, or issues related to life. Many of them arrive with an expectation that we will think for them so that they don't have to think for themselves.

As someone who works with youth and is equipping the next generation of youth pastors, this trend grieves me. Part of our worship is loving God with our minds. Worship is not just about our affections (emotions) or actions. Worship involves thinking about God and about the things of God. John Piper puts it this way: "So I take the word 'mind' in Matthew 22:37 to refer to that aspect of our being especially devoted to *thinking*. Loving God with all our mind means wholly engaging our thinking to do all it

---

1   William Hendrickson, *The Gospel of Mark* (Grand Rapids: Baker, 1975), 493.

can to awaken and express the heartfelt fullness of treasuring God above all things."[2]

Loving God with our minds involves studying the Scriptures and thinking of the biblical doctrines, truths, and principles held within them. This involves becoming serious interpreters of the text. We need to help our students develop into disciples who are like the Bereans in Acts of whom Luke wrote, "Now these Jews were more noble than those in Thessalonica; they received the word with all eagerness, examining the Scriptures daily to see if these things were so" (Acts 17:11). Parents and youth pastors need to encourage students to meditate on Scripture or to think deeply about a particular passage during the day. We must equip our students to think, throughout their day, of how a passage of Scripture applies to their lives and to the world around them.

Jonathan Edwards practiced such contemplation or meditation on Scripture. Describing one such instance of meditating upon a passage or truth of God, Edwards wrote:

> Once, as I rode out into the woods for my health, in 1737, having alighted from my horse in a retired place, as my manner commonly has been, to walk for divine contemplation and prayer, I had a view that for me was extraordinary, of the glory of the Son of God, as Mediator between God and man, and his wonderful, great, full, pure and sweet grace and love, and meek and gentle condescension. This grace that appeared so calm and sweet, appeared also great above the heavens. The person of Christ appeared ineffably excellent with an excellency great enough to swallow up all thought and conception—which continued, as near as I can judge, about an hour; which kept me the greater part of the time in a flood of tears and weeping aloud. I felt an ardency of soul to be, what I know not otherwise how to

---

2   John Piper, *Think: The Life of the Mind and the Love of God* (Wheaton, IL: Crossway, 2010), 85.

express, emptied and annihilated; to lie in the dust, and to be full of Christ alone; to love him with a holy and pure love; to trust in him; to live upon him; to serve and follow him; and to be perfectly sanctified and made pure, with a divine and heavenly purity. I have, several other times, had views very much of the same nature, and which have had the same effects.[3]

Focusing our minds on God and his Word helps us avoid distractions that fight for our attention. Helping students to love God with their minds also assists them in their fight against idols that might occupy their thoughts. What or who we think about most is what or who we worship. We are admonished as Christ followers, "Do not be conformed to this world, but be transformed by the renewal of your mind, that by testing you may discern what is the will of God, what is good and acceptable and perfect" (Rom. 12:2). When we come to Christ at conversion, our minds are transformed. We follow Christ as Lord over all of who we are, including our minds. As we help students love God with their minds, we are helping them to live the transformed life to which God has called them and discouraging them from building other idols in their thought life. Such transformation occurs when the Spirit teaches us through the Word of God. John Stott writes, "Although Paul does not here tell us how our mind becomes renewed, we know from his other writing that it is by a combination of the Spirit and the Word of God."[4]

In addition, loving God with our minds involves thinking deeply about how contemporary questions relate to Scripture. We need to help students think deeply about valid questions regarding their faith. Loving God with our minds involves dealing with doubts or challenges to our faith that we encounter. Parents and youth leaders

---

3 Jonathan Edwards, "Memoirs of Jonathan Edwards," in *The Works of Jonathan Edwards* (Carlisle: Banner of Truth Trust, 1974), 1:xlvii.

4 John Stott, *Romans: God's Good News for the World* (Downers Grove, IL: InterVarsity Press, 1994), 324.

enable students to love God with their minds by walking with them in the journey of developing answers to their questions. Some of these questions are: How do I know that the Bible is true? What evidence is there that Jesus was actually a real person? Are there other ways to gain access to God apart from Jesus? How did humanity start?

It's important that parents and youth pastors engage these types of questions with their students. Obviously, the Bible is the first source of authority to which we must turn for answers in matters of faith and life. We also have more than two thousand years of Christian apologetics that have posited answers to these types of questions. From Justin Martyr to Ravi Zacharias, Christian leaders have a plethora of apologists from which they can draw to help their students pursue truth and love God with their minds in this way.

Loving God with our minds is an act of worship. Students who practice the approach to loving God with their minds mentioned above will further solidify right belief (orthodoxy) regarding the Word of God and who God is. As they use their minds to explore the infinite vastness and goodness of God, their hearts will begin to grow more in love with him. Orthodoxy will lead to orthopathy.

Loving God with Our Souls

As we love God with our minds and meditate on him and his Word, our love for him grows. The love that started in our minds moves to our affections or emotions as we focus upon him and his Word. Regarding the sweetness of the Word of God, the Psalmist writes, "How sweet are your words to my taste, sweeter than honey to my mouth!" (Ps. 119:103). As the Word of God grows sweeter to us as we read it, it's subject, God, grows sweeter in our affections. Another Psalm mentions this relationship between our affections toward the Lord and our intake of the Word of God. David writes, "Blessed is the man who walks not in the counsel of the wicked, nor stands in the way of sinners, nor sits in the seat of scoffers; but his delight is in the law of the LORD, and on his law he meditates day and night" (Ps. 1:1–2). We cannot delight in the Word of God without delighting in the God of the Word.

When students delight in the Lord, he becomes the focus of their affections. Their love for him grows as they come to know him more through reading his love letter to them. Through the sanctifying work of the Holy Spirit in their lives, he becomes their focus and delight of their lives. They focus their worship and affections toward him. D. A. Carson describes this delight in the Lord stating, "We worship our Creator-God 'precisely because he is worthy *delightfully* so.' What ought to make worship delightful to us is not, in the first instance, its novelty or its aesthetic beauty, but its object. God himself is delightfully wonderful, and we learn to delight in him."[5]

There is a direct correlation between our love for God and our love for people around us. When we love God more, we love others more as well. People are made in the image of God (Gen. 1:26–27); therefore, they have inherent value. The more our students fall in love with Christ, the more they will love the people Jesus loves. God is love (1 John 4:8). Loving God and loving other people is an act of worship involving the affections, emotions, or souls of our students. In essence, it is orthopathy expressed in worship.

We cannot discuss the love and delight our students have for the Lord without mentioning our role in modeling joy, delight, and love for the Lord. Do your students see your love for God and your love for your neighbor in your worship? Do you reflect the joy of the Lord to them? Does God's love in you express itself toward them? As parents and youth leaders, we need to ask ourselves these questions in our efforts to grow our students' expression of orthopathy (right emotions) in worship.

Loving God with Our Strength

Loving God with our strength relates to our actions. Oftentimes, parents and youth leaders focus on what students do as the only aspect of their worship. For years, we have addressed their behavior without focusing on their minds and hearts. Understand that the discussion above regarding loving God with our minds and hearts (orthodoxy

---

5   D. A. Carson, *Worship by the Book* (Grand Rapids: Zondervan, 2002), 30.

and orthopathy) relates to our students' actions (orthopraxy). When students know God with their minds and love him more with their hearts, they will have a greater desire to follow his will in what they do.

It's important that we help our students understand how their actions are an act of worship. Worship is not just what we do corporately as a congregation. It's also not just having a daily time of Bible reading and prayer. Worship involves Christ followers living out, through their daily actions and interactions, the transformation the gospel has worked in their lives through the regenerating and sanctifying work of the Holy Spirit. Paul writes, "I appeal to you therefore, brothers, by the mercies of God, to present your bodies as a living sacrifice, holy and acceptable to God, which is your spiritual worship" (Rom. 12:1). Because we've been changed through the grace and mercy of Christ Jesus in the gospel, we are to live in a way that reflects that gospel. God has made us holy through the life, death, and resurrection of Christ Jesus; therefore, our holy lives should reflect the new creation that we are in Christ Jesus.

This living out of the gospel is an act of worship toward God that happens twenty-four hours a day, seven days a week in the life of the Christ follower. Our worship is not just a cerebral or emotional exercise. What we believe about God and the degree to which our affections are focused on him have a direct bearing on whether we will sacrifice our wills to follow his will in how we act. John Stott writes, "No worship is pleasing to God which is purely inward, abstract and mystical; it must express itself in concrete acts of service performed by our bodies."[6]

As we discussed in the chapter on orthopraxy, it is imperative that parents and youth leaders demonstrate to students what Christ followers do and why they do it. This is not moralistic therapeutic deism. It is not doing the right thing and living a moral life so that God will bless us. We must teach students that following Jesus Christ involves sacrificing ourselves on a daily basis out of our love and delight toward God and desire to follow and do his will. As new creatures in Christ, our love and wills have been changed. Though we formerly

6   Stott, *Romans,* 322.

loved ourselves alone, as Christ followers we yearn to love and know Christ more. While we formerly wanted to do our own will, Jesus is now the Lord of our lives as Christ followers; therefore, we want to submit our lives to his will. Adult leaders need to teach and demonstrate to students that the life of the Christ follower might involve suffering and being faithful to Christ in the absence of any recognizable or tangible earthly blessings. We must explain to students that the Christian life is not one of seeking to display a morality based on our efforts and energy, but instead it involves the Holy Spirit working in our transformed yet imperfect lives to conform us more into the image of Christ in our thoughts, affections, and actions. This sanctifying work of the Holy Spirit, in moving us to want to do what God wants and giving us the energy and discipline to do it, is evident in Paul's words to the church in Philippi. He writes, "Therefore, my beloved, as you have always obeyed, so now, not only as in my presence but much more in my absence, work out your own salvation with fear and trembling, for it is God who works in you, both to will and to work for his good pleasure" (Phil. 2:12–13). So it is wrong for us to teach mere morality. We need to paint an accurate picture of the Christian life reflecting in our actions, which are the outgrowth of a transformed life and the work of the Holy Spirit within the believer.

As with orthodoxy and orthopathy, it is vital that parents and youth leaders model orthopraxy as part of their worship to God. Students have problems resolving the veracity of our faith when they see adults whose words and actions do not match. They have problems when their parents claim the name of Christ but do not seek to honor him with their actions. Consistency between the gospel message we preach with our lips and the gospel message we live through our actions is imperative in helping students understand the relationship between the heart, mind, and actions of disciples of Jesus being unified in worship.

Family Worship

We have spent some time focusing on students' individual worship. We've explored the relationship between orthodoxy (mind), orthopathy (soul), and orthopraxy (strength) in individual worship. Through Paul's words to the churches in Rome and Philippi, we have reflected on individual worship being a 24-7 reality that grows from the daily life of the believer. As parents and youth leaders, we need to help students connect individual worship with family worship and corporate worship.

Family worship involves the guardian of the home, whether that be a parent or grandparent or someone else, leading the family in worship. These family worship gatherings might occur daily or weekly. I believe families should pray together daily and meet together for family worship at least once a week. During family worship, parents or guardians lead their students through a study of a passage of Scripture. It is a great opportunity for them to disciple their youth. Family worship should involve a time for family members to ask questions about a passage or particular topic related to their faith. They can discuss how a truth they are studying as a family applies to their lives at school, work, or home. These family worship times also offer youth a safe place to air their doubts about their faith. Family worship offers parents a powerful discipleship tool in the lives of their students.

For families to engage in this type of worship requires churches being proactive in leading lost parents to Christ and discipling them in the faith. Obviously, the youth pastor or youth ministry of the church cannot accomplish such a lofty goal alone. Church leaders and church members throughout the congregation must have a vision for reaching lost parents with the gospel and helping them grow in their faith so that they can disciple their students.

Youth pastors and youth leaders can place resources in the hands of parents to encourage parents in leading family worship.[7] Perhaps send a weekly devotional to parents that connects with what you are teaching in small group or youth worship. In these devotionals, list a focal passage and offer questions related to the passage that parents can use to guide their family worship. Ask the pastor to take a Sunday to model a family

---

7   One great resource for family worship is Donald S. Whitney's *Family Worship: In the Bible, in History, and in Your Home* (Wheaton, IL: Crossway, 2019).

worship service. During this worship service, have families roleplay family worship time, including the steps that the church leadership want to encourage families to take during their worship service. Some parents might not lead their families in worship because they've never seen it or experienced it. Such resources and examples can encourage parents to start having family worship in their homes.

Corporate Worship

Parents and church leaders must teach students that individual and family worship feeds into corporate worship. We need to help students participate in corporate worship, incorporating students into worship services as much as possible. Students need opportunities to use their spiritual gifts and God-given talents during the congregation's worship service. Such involvement in corporate worship helps remind students that they are not merely spectators but participants seeking to give the Lord glory and honor and praise along with the rest of the congregation. They are coming together with the congregation to praise the Lord on whom they have focused worship during their individual and family worship.

Those of us who lead youth have the awesome responsibility of teaching them how to worship—as individuals, with their families, and corporately. So, in relation to music in worship, what are some foundations today for corporate worship?

1. *Be biblical.* Youth may well get more theology from their songs than any source. It is fine to sing songs that touch the heart, but be sure to use songs that above all else teach biblical truth. Can you say that your youth often sing sound systematic theology?

2. *Be balanced.* The style of the service matters, make no mistake, and music can add a lot to style. But style is secondary to substance. And often overlooked in the style-over-substance debate is spirit. I have been in many contemporary services, and some were spirit-filled while others had no life—just fluff. I have also been in many traditional services. Some were dead

while others demonstrated great zeal for God. I personally prefer a more contemporary format, but that is simply my preference, and there is a difference between biblical values and personal preference.

3. *Be a part of the body.* Worship in such a way that speaks not only to the worshipers in your church, but that also connects them to the larger family of faith. In other words, it's fine to sing new songs, but also sing songs that maintain a heritage of the faith from generation to generation. Great hymns, for example, even when sung in a new way, do two things: first, they teach doctrine; second, they tie us to the best of the past. Dead tradition is a bad thing; maintaining a biblical heritage, however, is a good thing. When your students go to college, they should find a church with some songs they know.

4. *Be a blessing more than being blessed.* Many think the purpose of coming to a worship service is to be blessed, and worship can, indeed, offer a blessing. But the primary meaning of worship is to ascribe value, or worth, to another. Worship should focus more on being a blessing to God than on receiving blessings from him. Enough narcissism is in the church now. Teach youth to offer themselves to God as living sacrifices.

When students participate in the corporate worship services of their congregations, they have opportunity to interact in worship with Christ followers from other generations. This is an important part of corporate worship, worship involving people from each successive generation. Youth leaders must be careful that they do not allow a midweek youth worship service to substitute for the church's corporate service. By doing so, we create a parachurch within the congregation rather than encouraging unity in a youth group that is a vital part of the congregation. If you have a separate worship service for the youth, be sure that it encourages them to participate in the wider corporate service involving the entire congregation.

Another important aspect of worship is preaching. Whether preaching to students in the church's corporate service or preaching a worship service solely involving the youth group, pastors and youth pastors need to follow Paul's admonition to Timothy: "I charge you in the presence of God and of Christ Jesus, who is to judge the living and the dead, and by his appearing and his kingdom: preach the word; be ready in season and out of season; reprove, rebuke, and exhort, with complete patience and teaching" (2 Timothy 4:1–2). Students are hungry for the Word of God. They need to know how Scripture relates to the events and questions of the times. They need pastors and youth pastors who are well read regarding challenges to the faith coming from this post-Christian culture. We need to give them the Word to help them grow in their journey as disciples.

God is moving in some extraordinary ways throughout the fabric of this teen culture, and worship has become a vital part of the Christian young person's experience. It's not uncommon to find teens involved in worship gatherings of up to two hours long. The unrushed atmosphere spent seeking and waiting upon God allows these worshipers to heartily confess their sin to God, as well as drink in a sense of his forgiveness, grace, and mercy. Joy and enthusiasm of the Word of God sung and preached draw young people together.

Read Psalm 24:1–5. What kind of worshiper does God seek? Someone with clean hands, a pure heart. When you go to public worship on Sunday or to your youth meetings, do you take time to prepare your heart to encounter God? Here are three practical tips to make worship more meaningful. First, public worship comes from private worship. The more time you spend alone with God, the more authentic public worship becomes. Second, remember that worship is not primarily about you, it is about him. Keep your focus on him, and concentrate on honoring him. Finally, remember this whenever you worship: the more honest you are with God, the more real he will be to you. Open your heart to him, and experience the mighty presence of God.

God Is Looking for Worshipers

God is seeking true worshipers. Read John 4. He does not *need* worship. He *does* seek those who will worship him. With them, no matter their age, he can touch the world.

What did God do in the first century when he said, "I want one man to set the course for the early church"? He didn't pick Peter, James, and John, although he used them. He didn't pick any of the first twelve disciples. Instead, he found the most radical, fanatical man in the ancient Near East, Saul of Tarsus. And what was Saul doing? He was persecuting Christians. But after Saul met Jesus, God used him to lead the church. Why? I believe it was because he was the most passionate person anywhere. God just turned Saul's passion to himself.

When Saul, soon known as Paul, began to worship the living God, he touched the world. Once Paul was involved in ministry, people got tired of him and said, "Paul, we're going to kill you." Paul said, "To die is gain; absence from the body is presence with the Lord." They said, "We're going to make you happy, Paul; we'll let you live." He said, "Go ahead and let me live, I just want to preach. I'm not ashamed of the gospel." They said, "This is no good. I'll tell you what we'll do; we'll make you suffer." Paul said, "I know that the sufferings in this life are not worthy to be compared with the glory I'll see." These are not the attitudes of a lukewarm Christian; they're the attitudes of a fanatic.

Paul liked to worship, and his worship led him to witness. That's what happens when one encounters Jesus. When Jesus's followers met him after the resurrection, they worshiped (Matt. 28:16–20), and immediately he gave them the Great Commission—to witness. Worship led to witness in the life of Isaiah (Isa. 6), in the woman at the well (John 4), and in the early church (Acts 2:42–47).

If you truly worship God—not an experience, but God—it will cost you. If you stand for Jesus, it will cost you. But if you become a spiritual wimp who just serves Jesus when it's safe, it will cost you far more. You are not neutral—you're either nudging people toward Jesus, or you are nudging people toward hell.

A Romanian pastor who faced tremendous persecution by communists in his country observed that American Christianity speaks much of commitment but little of surrender. Yet Romans 12:1–2 focuses on surrendering our lives, not just adding Jesus to our little list of commitments. This pastor distinguished between commitment and surrender with a simple illustration. Imagine that you have a sheet of paper and a pen. That sheet of paper represents your life. A person who *commits* to follow Jesus writes down what he will do for Jesus—how much money he will spend, how much time he will give, and so on—and sign at the bottom, offering the sheet to the Lord.

Handing a written list over to the Lord may sound spiritual, but it actually means we call the shots for our life. In contrast, a person *surrendered* to the Lord will sign the bottom of the sheet while it's blank and then hand the sheet and the pen to Jesus, saying, "Lord, whatever You put on that sheet I will do." Worship means surrendering all we are to all he is in order to bring glory to his name.

Remember those twelve spies who were sent out by Moses? Ten of them came back with a negative report. They brought down a nation—a whole generation missed the promised land because ten people failed to trust God and surrender their lives and wills to him. Worship is *that* important.

11

ADVICE TO PARENTS
IT'S TIME TO GROW UP

Hear, O Israel: The LORD our God, the LORD is one! You shall love the LORD your God with all your heart, with all your soul, and with all your strength.

And these words which I command you today shall be in your heart. You shall teach them diligently to your children, and shall talk of them when you sit in your house, when you walk by the way, when you lie down, and when you rise up. You shall bind them as a sign on your hand, and they shall be as frontlets between your eyes. You shall write them on the doorposts of your house and on your gates.
—Deuteronomy 6:4–9

Does this family sound familiar?

It has been twelve days since Mom, Dad, Erich, Janey, and Melissa Morgan had a meal together. No, Dad isn't out of town, and no one is angry. They didn't plan it this way, but they figure that is just the way life is today.

You see, Erich's bus leaves for high school at 7:05 a.m. Janey leaves for middle school at 7:40. Mom takes Melissa to elementary school at 8:45 a.m., and then she's off to work. She works 3/4 time so she can be with the children—but in reality, the only time she is "with" the children is when she's in the van. She feels more like a taxi driver than a mom.

Janey, one of the top acrobatic and jazz dancers in her troupe, has advanced dance class after school on Monday, Tuesday, and Thursday until 6:00 p.m. (with an occasional Saturday morning rehearsal). Erich's high school basketball team, off to a two and seven start, is practicing overtime every day after school except on days when there are games. Melissa wants to be a dancer like Janey, so she practices with the beginner group, as soon as Janey's class is over.

Monday night is church visitation. Wednesday night there are church activities. Sunday night is church, too, of course. Almost every Friday or Saturday night at least one of the children is spending the night with a friend. And Saturday is lawn day, basketball games, dance performances . . . the list is endless. Mom is taking a computer course on Tuesday evenings. Some of Dad's clients insist on dinner meetings. There seem to be two or three a week.

Perhaps you recognize this family. Stretched, stressed, and losing touch with each other. This family is easy to find. It lives in your neighborhood, on your block, maybe in your house. . . . [But], you don't want to raise your family like the Morgans.[1]

This excerpt from *Family to Family* by Victor Lee and Jerry Pipes illustrates a realistic depiction of a churched family in America. If we are to raise a generation to serve God, changing this picture is critical. Why? Because the greatest impact in the life of youth is not made by their peers; the greatest impact in the life of youth is made by adults, and especially by parents. That's why effective youth ministers do not spend 90 percent of their time with

---

1   Victor Lee and Jerry Pipes, *Family to Family* (Atlanta: NAMB, 1999), 5.

students; instead, they spend about a third of their time with the students, a third of the time with parents and other significant adults, and a third of the time with all of them together. My first-year youth ministry students are surprised when I tell them that effective youth ministry is more about discipling parents and adult leaders than it is about discipling students. The students will be discipled by their parents and adult leaders in the youth group. This will be a radical change for most youth ministers, but one that will move youth to change the world for God.

Today's Parents Want to Get It Right

Youth pastors often complain that the biggest hindrance to raising the bar in youth ministry is parents. Many parents don't think of the long-term implications of a youth ministry that's based on silliness, yet it is the parents who cry the loudest when their children aren't having "fun." American youth have parents who grew up when being a parent too often meant being a "buddy" to children. The failure of parenting, and of marriages for that matter, has had a serious, negative impact on millions of youth. But if many of the problems facing youth begin with parents, the solution can begin there as well. And many children want their parents to make that change.

The members of Generation Z show a more conservative approach to their behavior than their parents' generations. They are less likely to drink alcohol than their parents. They are also less likely to have premarital sex. Youth who belong to Generation Z are also less likely to get into a fight at school than their parents' generation. Finally, they are less likely to argue with their parents than the Millennials or Generation X.[2]

Parents, how do you see youth ministry? Do you think that youth ministry primarily should provide activities for your children? If so,

---

2   Jean M. Twenge, *iGen: Why Super-Connected Kids Are Growing Up Less Rebellious, More Tolerant, Less Happy, and Completely Unprepared for Adulthood, and What That Means for the Rest of Us* (New York: Atria, 2017), 22, 36–37, 43–44, 150.

please take a day off work and take your child to a theme park. Over the past several years my work with youth and youth ministers has led me to a clear conviction: parents of youth need to rediscover the biblical teaching of Deuteronomy 6:4–9. According to God's Word, the primary place of spiritual training is not the church but the home! It is true that youth ministry can have a strong role in helping youth from lost families connect with both the church and other adults. But the very best youth ministry should be nothing more for *Christian* families than an aid, supporting, not leading.

The good news is that over the past decade parents as a group have increasingly shown a growing interest in getting it right with their children. And increasingly youth pastors focus on the long-term impact of the church's ministry to teens. Youth pastor Mark DeVries decided to take a radical approach: "I was, and still am, committed to taking whatever steps are necessary to accomplish the intended purpose of the student ministry of our church: to lead young people toward Christian adulthood." He adds, "In a youth culture under-girded by stable families and many available adults, the old model of youth ministries (isolating youth from the world of adults for an hour or two) worked fine. But in the current environment . . . the old model for youth ministry is no longer capable of carrying young people to Christian maturity."[3]

Often, once families arrive on the church campus, churches separate family members who are already not spending much time together. Timothy Paul Jones reveals some shocking statistics regarding churched families:

- More than half of parents said that their families never or rarely engaged in any sort of family devotional time. Of the minority that did practice some sort of family de-votions, one-fourth admitted that these devotional times were sporadic.

---

3   Mark DeVries, "What Is Youth Ministry's Relationship to the Family?" in *Reaching a Generation for Christ* (Chicago: Moody, 1997), 480.

- Approximately 40 percent of parents never, rarely, or only occasionally discussed spiritual matters with their children.
- Nearly one-fourth of parents never or rarely prayed with their children; another one-fourth only prayed with their children occasionally.
- More than one-third of parents with school-aged children had never engaged in any form of family devotional or worship times at any time in the past couple of months. For an additional three out of ten parents, such practices occurred once a month or less.
- Among two-thirds of fathers and mothers, biblical discussions or readings with their children happened less than once each week.
- One in five parents never read, studied, or discussed God's Word with their children.[4]

In the midst of this disengagement regarding parents discipling their youth, teens want strong relationships with their parents. Members of Generation Z are less likely to fight with their parents or run away from home.[5] Mark DeVries writes, "With one in four young people now indicating that they have *never* had a meaningful conversation with their father, is it any wonder that 76 percent of the 1,200 teens surveyed in *USA Today* actually *want* their parents to spend more time with them."[6]

DeVries's observations parallel my research. As a youth pastor, pastor, and someone who speaks to youth groups on a regular basis, I've spoken to numerous teens and their families over the past few years. I have never encountered a parent who wanted to be a terrible parent. I have spoken with countless parents who want to do the right thing. Deuteronomy 6:4–9 offers timeless guidance for parents, but

---

4   Timothy Paul Jones, *Family Ministry Field Guide: How Your Church Can Equip Parents to Make Disciples* (Indianapolis: Wesleyan, 2011), 27–29.
5   Twenge, *iGen,* 44.
6   Mark DeVries, *Family-Based Youth Ministry* (Downers Grove, IL: InterVarsity Press, 2004), 41.

the way most Christian parents try to raise their children diverges radically from this biblical passage. Today, even the best-intentioned parents spend their time dealing with *behavior,* when what they should focus on is *belief.*

Deuteronomy 6:4–5, one of the most quoted passages in the Bible, begins with a statement of belief: *God is one.* Period. End of discussion. Are we teaching this fact to our children—that everything in life comes under the authority of the one, great, awesome, loving, holy God? The passage goes on to say that parents are to *teach* truth to their children. How? By saying it and by living it—when you walk in the way, when you sit in your house, when you rise. In other words, Christianity lived only on Sundays will never change the world for your children or others. We as parents must raise the bar in our Christian living!

The word *we* refers to both moms *and* dads. Robert Lewis makes this stirring, and accurate, observation: a cultural revolution has begun. What college students were to the 1960s, what women were to the 1970s, and what yuppies were to the 1980s, dads may be to the 1990s and beyond. Fathers are coming home. And it is not just within the ranks of evangelical Christianity. The revolution transcends religious, racial, and ethnic boundaries.[7]

Here are a few practical tips to help move your family to a Deuteronomy 6 model:

1. *If you don't control your time, someone else will.* Angela and I did not have our first children, twin sons, until we were in our late twenties and early thirties. Up until that point, we observed parents who basically served as taxi drivers for their kids, taking them from ball practice to dance to church to karate. So many families were exhausted, going from activity to activity. So, while our kids were still small, we decided that our kids would choose one activity each season. In the winter they played basketball. In the fall they tried football.

---

7   Robert Lewis, *Raising a Modern-Day Knight* (Wheaton, IL: Tyndale House, 1997), 37–38.

In the spring they played soccer. The point is that we were more committed to our time as a family than we were sports or other activities in which our children were involved. You cannot implement the lived-out faith of Deuteronomy 6 when you're exhausted from behaving more like taxi drivers than parents. We tried to set the standard early that Mom and Dad, not activities, would set the calendar.

2. *Make time to do what is important*—like faithful attendance in worship, family times of devotion or family worship, like times to get away as a family, and like regular family nights and meals together.

3. *Men, give your wife and kids the very best of your discretionary time.* We live incredibly busy lives. I travel a lot, both overseas and in the states. My wife and kids know I'd rather be with them than anywhere else on the planet. When I was deployed on Operation Noble Eagle and Operation Enduring Freedom, I never regretted not spending more time at work. I did regret not spending enough time with my family. You will never get time back. Once the seconds, minutes, hours, days, months, and years are spent, they are gone. Spend time with your family. You won't regret it.

4. *Every day, do something in your children's world.* I'm a professor at a fast-growing, incredibly hectic university. As I write this chapter, I have got another book I need to start on next week. I am the director of the Global Center for Youth Ministry, doing youth ministry around the planet. I am the lead pastor and planter of a multiethnic, multigenerational church plant. Yet the most important roles I play are husband to my wife and father to our four children. I try to make a habit of spending time with my kids on a regular basis. Sometimes this looks like taking them out to breakfast individually on a Saturday morning. Sometimes it means taking a walk with them and talking with them. On other occasions, it means having one of them go with me to a speaking event (I rotate this opportunity between the kids). This quality time with my kids keeps

me in their world, even if it looks like singing '80s music driving home from a speaking event with my oldest daughter.

5. *Discover what your kids love to do, and regularly do it with them.* That shows your kids that they matter to you. Take your daughter roller-skating. Shoot hoops with your son. It is okay if you are pitiful at it; if your child loves doing it, spend time doing it with your child. I teach and train in martial arts with all of my children on a weekly basis. We have been training together for the last eight years. They wanted to take martial arts, so I took with them to spend time with them.

Showing your kids that you care can be done in very practical ways in the home. Sit at the foot of the bed longer. Eat meals together. Go to ball games. Sacrifice for them. Discipline them. And, as mentioned, find out what is important to them and do it with them. Do you even know what things are most important to your children? If not, put this book down and find out. Do it now, especially if your children are young, because if you wait until they are seventeen, you have missed your window of opportunity.

The Desire of Youth

I had a young man in one of our classes who had a very strained relationship with his father. I found out that his father was a well-educated pastor. His father had received a terminal degree and written a dissertation on a hero of the faith who is considered one of the greatest theologians in America.

The young man told me how his dad could and would speak hours about this hero theologian. He would share with passion minute details about the man's life, history, and contribution to the church. This pastor/father would speak with his son about the man's impact upon his ministry as a pastor.

What was telling was that this young man never spoke of a conversation where his father actually took an interest in him. I realize I only received one side of the story, but this son spoke of a father who never really discussed the Scriptures or discipled him. He had time for his own discipleship and time to disciple the members of the church, but when it came to his son, it seemed he did not have the interest or the time. He also spoke of a dad who never threw a football with him or did things together with him that he enjoyed doing.

The tone of this young man's voice betrayed a bitterness toward as father who spoke of shepherding and loving the church but did not take the time to shepherd and love his son. He did not discuss theological matters with him to see where he was in his spiritual journey. This young man's dad never helped him navigate the doubts he had regarding the faith or study to find answers in Scripture to some of the harder questions related to the faith. Unfortunately, the young man's professors served in that role in his life. This young student saw his dad as a hypocrite who would shepherd the church but not his own son.

Your kids want you in their lives. But if years of communication problems have built up walls, it will take time to tear them down. And if you think your teenager loathes the very thought of being around you, think again. The members of Generation Z want to have good relationships with their parents. Sometimes they push back because their parents are so overprotective; however, this is not a reaction to a lack of desire for relationship with mom and dad. It is the normal process within the life of a teenager of wanting support while, at the same time, learning how to become more independent. "Family is a big deal to teenagers, regardless of how they act or what they say," Barna observed. "It is the rare teenager who believes he or she can lead a fulfilling life without receiving complete acceptance and support from his or her family." Barna discovered, in fact, that "in spite of the seemingly endless negative coverage in the media about the state of the family these days, most teens are proud of their family. Nine out of 10 (90 percent) consider their family to be 'healthy and functional.' This is an extraordinarily high figure given that one-third of the teens interviewed are living in either a 'blended' or 'broken' home—i.e., a home situation in which they are not living with both of their natural parents."[8] Regarding the desire of teens to spend time with their parents and family, *Science Daily* reports, "Teenagers are famous for seeking independence from their parents, but research shows that many teens continue to spend time with their parents and that this shared time is important for teens' well-being, according to Penn State researchers."[9]

Teenagers seek the respect of their parents. Teenagers wish their parents would be more trusting that their teens were capable of making good decisions. They wish, too, that their parents would better understand the strengths of teens. Barna also learned that, in surveys, youth scored their parents low on following through with commitments. Teens notice when parents do not keep their promises. Still, Barna's research shows that the people the teens spend the most time with— their friends—were the least likely to give them a sense of peace. Rather, the people that gave them the most sense of peace were their parents.[10]

Ruth Bell Graham, the wife of Billy Graham, is said to have given this advice to parents: When your children are young, teach them; when they're older, listen to them. Today, however, youth spend an average of three and one-half hours alone each day, and 63 percent of youth live in homes where both parents work. Who, then, is teaching and listening to these kids? As Josh McDowell puts it, "When young people don't feel that you identify with them, they are less likely to stay connected emotionally to you."[11]

In *The Disconnected Generation*, McDowell offers six areas where parents can and must connect with their children:

- Affirmation—giving youth a sense of authenticity
- Acceptance—giving youth a sense of security

---

8   George Barna, *Real Teens: A Contemporary Snapshot of Youth Culture* (Ventura, CA: Regal, 2001), 68.

9   Penn State, "Time with Parents Is Important for Teens' Well-Being," *ScienceDaily*, www.sciencedaily.com/releases/2012/08/120821143907.htm.

10 Barna, *Real Teens*, 77.

11 Josh McDowell, *The Disconnected Generation* (Nashville: Word, 2000), 48, also 10.

- Appreciation—giving youth a sense of significance
- Affection—giving youth a sense of lovability
- Availability—giving youth a sense of importance
- Accountability—giving youth a sense of responsibility

What Can a Church Do?

If the parents are believers, the primary place of spiritual nurture and training for children should be the home, with the church accenting and enhancing this teaching. If Christian parents assumed spiritual responsibility for their children, more church resources could be focused on assisting youth from non-Christian homes. These youth need huge amounts of teaching, love, and encouragement.

How selfish it would be, then, for even parents who are most active in the church to expect youth ministry to revolve around their children! Yet I see this "church is a hotel for saints, not a hospital for sinners" mentality all too often.

Still, churches can and do teach biblical principles on raising children to adulthood. Most churches feature sermon series on the family or sponsor parenting conferences. Should churches not also teach parents how to lead their children to Christ? When was the last time that you heard a pastor or a children's minister teach on how parents can lead their children to Christ? Nothing should be more important to a Christian parent than to see his or her child come to Christ, yet the church seldom, if ever, teaches parents how to evangelize to their children. Maybe our sermons and conferences on parenting are missing the point.

Parents, it is time for us to come back to the priority of the Christian home. We need to help our teenagers learn how to become disciples. It starts when they are children.

Discipling our kids means that we need to put our smartphones down and focus on our children. They need to have our attention. Too many parents allow portable electronic devices to parent their children and teenagers. The youth today need parents who are willing to be different. In a culture where time on the internet and social media is causing us to become isolated and separate, parents need to stand in the gap and provide the type of authentic personal relationship that cannot be found virtually. We need to be parents and not bystanders who watch our teens slide into depression because they are comparing themselves and their lives to the fake personas they see online. Are you willing to be *that parent?* My wife and I give our kids time limits on their smartphones and the internet. They are not allowed to take their phones to bed. We have a charging station in the living room where they deposit their phones before they go to bed. No cell phones are allowed at the table. Yes, we actually have meals together where we talk with each other. My wife and I realize that no one else will set healthy parameters on our kids' use of cell phones. It's our responsibility to parent and love them enough to pursue authentic gospel-centered discipleship relationships with our kids.

Part of our parenting in relation to the internet and portable electronic devices includes us protecting our students from adults who try to profit by seeking our teenagers' harm. James Emery White sounds this sobering warning:

> Being the first generation with a connection to the internet in their pocket has, as you would imagine, its dark side—namely, the ubiquitous presence and availability of pornography. No other generation has had pornography so available, in such extremes, at such a young age. Seventy percent of all eighteen-to thirty-four-year-olds are regular viewers. The average age to begin viewing? Eleven.[12]

It is irresponsible and unloving for parents not to help their kids navigate the internet in such a way that sets boundaries through filters and accountability software. A simple search online reveals Christian filtering plans that are both affordable and available to protect teenagers' computers and portable electronic devices. Parents need to

---

12   James Emery White, *Meet Generation Z: Understanding and Reaching the New Post-Christian World* (Grand Rapids: Baker, 2017), 58.

protect their students from adults who seek to make monetary profit by exposing our youth to such harmful content online.

Evaluate How Adults See Youth

Many parents view the teen years as no more than a horrible period they must somehow suffer through. Enough of this. Yes, they are challenging years. Yes, they take much work and prayer. But they are also full of opportunities to guide our children into the adult world.

Parents, how do you see your children? I agree with David Black, who argues that parents are to expect the best, not the worst, from their children. Assuming they will turn out badly, rearing them to focus incessantly on what could go wrong with their lives, can become a self-fulfilling prophecy. "If we expect them to act like irresponsible children, they will," Black states. "On the other hand, if we expect them to act like responsible adults, as people did for thousands of years, they will."[13]

Barna's research found the following: "While adults, especially in the media, have a tendency to refer to teenagers as pessimistic, 'slackers' and self-absorbed, teens resent such depictions."[14] Seven adjectives describing teens were chosen to show what teens believed adults thought of them. Five of the seven are negative: lazy, rude, sloppy, dishonest, and violent. The two positive ones were: friendly and intelligent. "Naturally, few teens view themselves or their generation in such negative terms," Barna observed. "However, such a projection helps to explain why teens struggle with taking directions from, or being educated by, adults: They do not believe that adults respect, understand them or give the freedom and creative license that they desire."[15]

Certainly, teenagers with their hormonal changes and their developing minds have a rebellious streak in them—no doubt about it.

---

13 David Alan Black, *The Myth of Adolescence* (Yorba Linda, CA: Davidson, 1998), 21.
14 Barna, *Real Teens*, 54.
15 Barna, *Real Teens*, 54.

But parents inadvertently often encourage that rebellious streak by treating teenagers like fourth-graders. Perhaps we should try, instead, respecting them and listening to them. I'm weary of hearing youth tell me that they feel adults consider youth to be a nuisance in the church.

Churches help to reinforce this perception. For many students, their only opportunity to help exercise their gifts in the congregational worship service is the annual Youth Sunday that occurs in churches. It is usually a worship service led once a year by the students. Often it is held on Sunday night because the churches do not trust the students with a Sunday morning service. Pastors in these same churches will talk about the youth being the future of the church. That is the problem. They don't understand that, as Christ followers, believing students are part of the church right now. No wonder students leave the church after they graduate from high school. They never felt like they were part of it when they were there. Churches need to trust youth with ministry, responsibility, and opportunities to exercise their spiritual gifts in ministry. We need to raise the bar.

Parents also help to reinforce this stereotype of youth being unable to lead out as growing and maturing Christ followers. As a professor of youth ministry and missions, I encounter numerous prospective and incoming students who are excited about God's call to ministry in their lives. They have a sense of anticipation of how God will use them to help make an impact for the kingdom of Christ and the advancement of the gospel. They have a willingness to go anywhere and take any risk to reach people who have never heard the name of Jesus with the hope of the gospel message. I listen to this excitement in their voices as they share their stories when I meet them. Then their parents start talking. Now as a parent, I understand some of their concerns regarding finances and employment; however, many parents I encounter are actually less mature spiritually than their teenage students. Their students have faith that the Lord has called them to ministry and will provide for their needs as they pursue his call upon their lives; however, the parents talk about changing majors to one that helps provide a "safety net" or "fall back plan" when this "ministry thing" doesn't work out. Let me note, these parents are self-professed Christ followers and church members. Students speak with passion about reaching unengaged unreached people groups with the gospel. Then the parents talk about the danger of the mission field and the lack of money they will make when they are overseas.

Parents, we need to be sure that we are not holding our students back from leading and pursuing the call of God upon their lives. Rather, we need to walk beside them as they follow Christ and hold them with open hands. We are simply stewards of these precious children God has given us to help raise them into the disciples he has called them to be to deploy them for his kingdom work.

Besides at home and in church, another place that youth should be learning these skills is in school. I'm a radical on education, and I'm not alone. Specialists in various fields are looking at the needs of adolescents and asking whether the nation's high schools are meeting them. Many experts believe that by not challenging teenagers' considerable powers—which are often equal to those of adults—and by not building on their desire to connect with the adult world, high schools all too often place students in a motivational vacuum. Combine that with conditions at odds with the teenage body—early start times, too little sleep, too much seat time—and educators on the front lines are confronted with a formidable challenge. The result is that too many schools are losing too many students—if not in body, then in mind and spirit.

Many researchers make the point that by age fifteen or so, youth are in many ways the physical and mental equals—even superiors—of adults. Older teenagers are at their lifetime peak for such characteristics as speed, reaction time, and memory. They are also generally more daring than adults. Leon Botstein—president of Bard College in Annandale-on-Hudson, New York, and a critic of American high schools—argues that recent phenomena in human biology play a role in teenagers' dissatisfaction with high school. Today's teenagers, Botstein says, typically reach puberty two or three years earlier than their counterparts at the beginning of the twentieth century and so, by the end of high school, have had the physical hallmarks of adult men and women for several years.[16]

Considering the ambitions and the physical, mental, and spiritual capabilities of youth, doesn't it seem that the teen years are the ideal time to teach these kids to be leaders?

The Place of Youth Ministry: Entertainers or Role Models?

I've had the opportunity to interact with a number of awesome youth pastors who point their students to Jesus. They work hard to come alongside parents and adult leaders to help them lead and disciple students. They have been discipling parents, adult leaders, and students for twenty to thirty years and are still going strong in youth ministry in their fifties. Unfortunately, I've also run into numerous leaders in youth ministry who seem to believe that their role is to entertain students in an attractional model where they are the best entertainers, and their churches are the best entertainment centers in the area. They dumb down students and dumb down the gospel because of this inaccurate and demeaning perception of teenagers. Because of their unbiblical and unhealthy view of youth ministry, they look down on older youth pastors.

When some of these entertainment guys meet me, they are shocked that I'm still speaking to students and writing books about youth ministry at the age of forty-nine. How could I still possibly communicate effectively to teenagers? Such a false assumption does not encourage youth to plan far ahead for a life of service to God. I thank God for the youth pastors I know who are still youth-ministry giants in their fifties. They are committed to raising the bar in youth ministry. I cannot depend on them, however, to be my children's primary discipler. I'm the one who is primarily responsible for being my students' (kids) *main* pastor.

Who, though, will minister to youth whose families are nonbelievers? While the role of youth ministry is to give biblical emphasis

---

16   Bess Keller, "Schools Seen as Out of Sync with Teens," *EdWeek*, May 2, 2001, https://www.edweek.org/ew/articles/2001/05/02/33develop.h20.html.

for strengthening Christian families in the church, a further role is to evangelize to the families of the youth who attend. How many youth pastors or ministries would boast that in a given year, scores of youth from unchurched homes attend their church, but those same ministers give virtually no attention to reaching those parents? What could be more important to the future of those youth than to see their parents come to Christ?

In terms of strengthening Christian families, I'm not advocating the position that a twenty-three-year-old youth pastor should teach parents how to raise their teens. But that pastor can show youth how to walk with God, can teach the Word, and can provide resources—such as strong Christian families as examples—to aid other families.

Involve Significant Adults

What more vital role could older adults have in the church than to take under their wing a student from an unsaved family? Multitudes of young people come from lost homes and may themselves be lost. We must challenge older adults to pour their lives into such young adults. Some of the greatest influences in the lives of my children have been men and women the age of their grandparents. One couple in their seventies or eighties in my church are retired missionaries who spent thirty years planting churches and doing medical missions in Africa. They encourage my kids in their faith and speak words of love to them on a regular basis. My teenagers listen intently to the stories of how God worked through them when they were on the field. They see how God is using them to feed hungry people in our community and help us to plant a multiethnic multigenerational church in a small city in the South. By sharing their stories and living out God's call on their lives in ministry, these senior adults are speaking into the faith stories of my teenage children. These are the types of adults I want doing youth ministry.

Richard R. Dunn uses the acronym SOAP—Significant Other Adult Person—to refer to "those important mentors who can make all the difference in . . . maturation." How, though, do churched youth, as well as newly converted youth, connect with a SOAP if young people are continually funneled into youth programs? "Youth leaders in local churches must guard against developing youth ministries that are 'mini parachurches.' Parachurch leaders likewise face the challenge of connecting converts to local church fellowships." Dunn recognizes that failure to address these concerns can lead to two negative results: "First, in the present, students miss the rich spiritual heritage of intergenerational relationships in the body of Christ. Second, in the future, students lacking meaningful connections to the broader faith community often drop out of church following high school graduation."[17]

Youth pastors, then, have a formidable responsibility. People criticize, with some justification, that many youth ministries today seem to be built on entertainment. But the truth is, whatever you're doing, if you see no change in your students over time, you are merely entertaining them, not mentoring them.

A seven-year-old went through his parents' devastating divorce. For months after the divorce he was wetting his pants. His father tried everything to correct the problem. He read books. He took his son to the doctor. He sent off for programs. Nothing worked. Finally, the father sat down with his son and asked, "What's going on? Babies do this."

The boy answered, "And their daddies hold them."

Children of all ages need adults. What if parents are AWOL? What about students in your church whose parents do not care about the things of God? Involving adults, whether parents or not, is vital to the development of youth in the church. DeVries hits the mark when he asks:

> Where do hurting students turn for their most significant long-term health? In her fascinating book, *Children of Fast Track Parents,* A. A. Brooks documents, "Studies of resiliency

---

17   Richard R. Dunn, "Putting Youth Ministry into Perspective," in *Reaching a Generation of Christ,* eds. Richard R. Dunn and Mark H. Centers III (Chicago: Moody, 1997), 65.

in children show time and again that consistent emotional support of at least one loving adult can help children overcome all sorts of chaos and deprivation." Urie Bronfrenbrenner's declaration, "Somebody's got to be crazy about the kid," points to the heart of family-based youth ministry. *Perhaps the best gift a youth ministry can give teenagers is not to impress them or attract them, but to ensure that each young person has an adult in the church who delights in him or her.* The church family becomes the family base."[18]

It is a sad fact of life that often the stronger the youth program in the church, and the more deeply the young people of the church identify with it, the weaker the chances are that those same young people will remain in the church when they grow too old for the youth program. Why? Because the youth program has become a substitute for participation in the church. . . . When the kids outgrow the youth program, they also outgrow what they have come to know of the church.[19]

As I type this, we are experiencing a pandemic in our country that has caused my university to move our classes from a traditional seated format to an online platform. I spent this morning advising college students through a video teleconferencing app. I'm listening to country music on Spotify streaming on the internet. Next to me on my desk, my cell phone vibrates because my news app is sending me notifications about the condition of the virus in my state. My watch is measuring my pulse and telling me when I need to stand up and move around.

We have so many ways to communicate. We have been blessed with technology like the world has never seen. But the technology has failed to bring human beings closer together. Technology does not guarantee intimacy. It may, in fact, hinder intimacy due to the distraction it brings. People, especially young people, need intimacy in relationships.

---

18 DeVries, "What Is Youth Ministry's Relationship to the Family?" 494.
19 Ben Patterson, in DeVries, "What Is Youth Ministry's Relationship to the Family?" 493.

Perhaps that explains why many youth organizations that were begun by older adults have failed. Barna notes, "Too few organizations have effectively rallied young people around the vision, a cause or purpose, that might ordinarily appeal to young adults: more often than not, those organizations are led by adults perceived to hold negative views about teens and young adults. Without a sense of acceptance and respect, young people are not prone to submitting themselves to the leadership of people or organizations who failed to embrace them as people."[20]

Acceptance and respect are the secrets to Greg Stier and his Dare 2 Share ministry. Thousands, sometimes tens of thousands, gather in huge arenas to hear Greg preach to young people about how they are the hope for the future. He has a vision for teenagers throughout the United States to reach their peers with the gospel. Greg's vision is successful because he believes in young people, and he challenges them to do great things for God, like reaching that lost friend with the gospel.

The first institution God created was not the church. It was not government. It was the family. And the family lies at the very heart of the church's task today—helping parents lead their children and raise their children to be champions for God who advance the gospel and the kingdom of Christ.

---

20   Barna, *Real Teens*, 57.

12

MEANWHILE, BACK AT THE CHURCH
STAFF RELATIONS AND LEADING A MINISTRY

> And he gave the apostles, the prophets, the evangelists, the shepherds and teachers, to equip the saints for the work of ministry, for building up the body of Christ.
>
> —Ephesians 4:11–12

Youth pastors, if we're going to raise the bar of how we do youth ministry, many of the leaders in our churches need to change the way we do ministry together. I have had the privilege of serving in small, medium, and large churches. In every one of these church environments, I have witnessed the same challenges that can prevent churches from making Christ followers of people from every generation, young to old. Church staff members often think of their own ministry area without seeing their church from a larger perspective. A number of these staffers know their ministry areas well but never stop to think about how their ministry fits into the broader life of the body of Christ. Sometimes, leaders of church ministries fight turf wars with each other, competing over volunteers or funding. Such in-fighting and lack of seeing the big picture occurs also in churches that are too small to pay staff members to lead each ministry area.

Another challenge I've seen relates to a perspective that the pastors and ministers of the church are the hired guns who are responsible for doing ministry and sharing the gospel. Many church members would never say it, but they do not feel the responsibility to make disciples or minister because "that's what we're paying the staff to do." They do not see themselves as ministers or ambassadors of Christ deployed to spread the gospel and advance the kingdom of Christ throughout their communities and the world. Rather than players in the game, these church members are spectators in the stands.

These challenges prompt several questions: Are the leaders of the church unified regarding the mission of their church and the role they play in that mission? Do they see themselves as professional hired guns responsible for growing their respective ministry areas or as leaders within the same body called to equip Christ followers from every generation to deploy as ministers and lights in a dark world that desperately needs Jesus?

Also, within this conversation, regarding youth ministry, the next generation needs youth pastors who know their biblical role within the body of Christ and work well together with their pastors, fellow staff members, parents, adult leaders, and student leaders to engage the next generation and its family members with the gospel. They need to be servant leaders who point people who are following them to follow Jesus.

In short, the above conversation has one dynamic in common— church leadership. How should church leaders work together to do effective ministry that engages students and their families?

A Word to Pastors and Youth Pastors

Having served as both a youth pastor and a lead pastor, allow me to speak a word to lead or senior pastors. Pastors, I want to encourage you to live out the biblical role to which God called you in relation to your church leaders and staff members. God did not call you to be a CEO. He did not call you to be a rancher or a coach. As pastors, God called you to serve as under shepherds who follow the example of the Good Shepherd, Jesus Christ, in their leadership. God has called you to be servant leaders who lead with grace and humility. As shepherds, he has called you to feed, nurture, and protect the sheep. Within the church, your church leaders and staff are the first part of the flock you need to shepherd. You are accountable for the soul care you provide for your staff.

You need to feed your church leaders and staff and teach them how to feed themselves. Disciple your staff members. Use staff meetings as a time to focus them upon the Word of God and how it impacts their leadership in the church. In the context of this book, help your youth pastors to be students of God's Word. Disciple them. When they have a conversation with you, your youth pastors should leave with a deeper desire to read, understand, and apply the Word of God.

You need to nurture your youth pastors and staff members. Pastors, if you call youth pastors, support them. If they are young, mentor them. In the past, young people called to the ministry served as apprentices to other ministers. Today that tradition is largely lost, although some pastors of larger churches have revived an intern ministry. Instead, most youth pastors begin ministry in their twenties. They still need a pastor to guide them, to teach them how to be youth *pastors,* not *youth* pastors. They need your help learning how to make disciples, provide pastoral care, handle conflict, manage finances, lead meetings, make a calendar, and a plethora of the other responsibilities involved in their ministries. And they certainly need a pastor to support them. Don't hire a youth pastor just to get the youth ministry out of your hair or the parents off your back.

Pastors need to protect their youth pastors and staff. Your youth pastors and staff need to know you have their back. They need the freedom to be creative and even fail without fear of unnecessary rebuke or termination. Help them achieve ministry goals by encouraging them, providing the resources they need, and holding them accountable to the goals they have set. Doing these things protects them by helping them as they seek to lead their teams in ministry. For young youth pastors, pastors need to either disciple parents regarding their parenting or provide someone who can speak authoritatively to parents regarding raising teenagers. Otherwise, parents often will look at the young youth pastor and ask the question, "What could you possibility teach me about being a parent when you've never done it?" Pastors protect young youth pastors from their students' parents by being sensitive to this potential problem in their ministry.

Pastors, these are only a few ideas of how you can feed, nurture, and protect your youth pastors and staff members.

Youth pastors, sometimes you complain that you are treated like second-class ministers, not quite up to the standard of "real" ministry. So you are patronized and too often not taken seriously. You may, however, perpetuate such a mentality by your behavior. I've seen youth pastors who didn't begin preparing their Bible study until thirty minutes before it was supposed to happen. When invited to speak at their Disciple Nows or camps, I've had them wait until the last minute to create or send me a schedule with a theme or desired sermon topics. They have failed to return my calls, emails, and even once failed to send an honorarium for an event. It wasn't about the money; it was about the failure on the part of the youth pastor to assume responsibility and pay attention to details. So, if you're a youth pastor, it's an unfortunate reality that you may have to work harder to be taken seriously as a minister. However, do not make the task more difficult by being unable to manage a calendar or make a meeting on time. If you want to dress like a teenager, fine, but do not complain when adults treat you like one. If we're to raise the bar, it starts with us—the ones who are in authority over youth. We are pastors. Let's act like it. It will make our lead pastors' jobs easier.

The Pastor and the Youth Pastor Are a Team

Youth pastor and pastor, find ways to encourage one another, to build up each other's ministry in the church you both serve. Youth pastor, involve your pastor whenever possible with the youth. Ask him at least once or twice a year to speak to your students. One pastor, who had formerly spent years in youth ministry, shared a valuable lesson. After hiring a sharp youth pastor, he basically forgot about that whole area of his church. Then his youth pastor invited him to speak to the youth on a Wednesday night. Afterward, the pastor was amazed at the number of e-mails he received from students in the church, and how they began to speak to him on Sundays. Young people often get the idea that they do not matter, and some pastors unintentionally give that impression.

Notice what Barna discovered about teens, church, and pastors.[1] Teens were given a list of eighteen factors related to church and were asked to choose which were most important to them. The number-one factor related to the people and their friendliness. The second related to the sermon quality and the theological beliefs of the church (two-thirds of teens consider that critical). Third was liking the pastor—not the youth pastor, but the *pastor.* Half of young people indicated that the pastor was important to them. Of interest, Barna found the least important factors were how far the church was from home, the length of the sermons, and the availability of small groups.

Pastors, youth pastors, staff members, and ministry leaders—to do intergenerational ministry, you must work as a team. The children's ministry, youth ministry, and adult ministry are all ministering to families. Children's ministers and youth ministers need to communicate regarding how to develop orthodoxy, orthopathy, and orthopraxy in the children and youth. How do the children's and youth ministries work together to help children transition to the youth group? How is the adult ministry helping parents to disciple their students? How are the adults in the church reaching lost parents of teenagers with the gospel? These are all questions that the ministries in the church need to work together to answer.

Models of Youth Ministry: Youth Ministry or Not?

Engaging Generation Z challenges the church to examine how we view youth and to set a higher standard in the fundamental ways we minister to them and to their families. It is the intent of *Engaging Generation Z,* then, to encourage and challenge you to expect more from and offer more to youth.[2] *Engaging Generation Z* is not, how-

---

1 George Barna, *Real Teens: A Contemporary Snapshot of Youth Culture* (Ventura, CA: Regal, 2001), 139.

2 Resources to help think through the big picture of youth ministry include Mark DeVries, *Family-Based Youth Ministry* (Downers Grove, IL: InterVarsity Press, 2004); Doug Fields, *Purpose-Driven Youth Ministry* (Grand Rapids: Zondervan, 1998); Timothy Paul Jones, *Family Ministry Guide* (Indianapolis: Wesleyan, 2011); Andy Stanley and Stuart Hall, *The Seven Checkpoints* (West Monroe, LA: Howard, 2001).

ever, a "how-to" book on the nuts and bolts of organizing a youth ministry nor an endorsement of any particular approach to student ministry (although I've identified ministries that, in my opinion, get it right). Rather, the challenge is, on the one hand, to focus on the big picture—the general philosophy of ministering to youth in the church today—and on the other hand to focus on the bottom line of witness, worship, Bible teaching, prayer, and theology.

Yet a major issue of contemporary youth ministry concerns its very existence. Numerous books, articles, and websites have been written or launched examining the level to which a church should be involved in youth ministry. And segregation by age within our churches is, indeed, a thorny issue. In the Western church, the whole concept of youth ministry is being reevaluated, and with good reason. The failure of youth ministry to produce a generation of strong, young adult believers has created strong reactions. Some advocate the abolition of such age segregation and thus the elimination of youth ministry.

It is beyond the scope of this book to address in depth the issue of age segregation versus integration. The best discussion I have seen on the matter is found in Timothy Paul Jones's book *Family Ministry Field Guide*. He describes four models churches generally use in ministering to families:

1. *Segmented-Programmatic Ministry Model*: Ministries are organized in separate "silos" with little consistent intergenerational interaction. Family ministry, if it exists, is simply one more program. The program may provide training, intervention, or activities for families. In scheduling programs, churches may deliberately seek to be sensitive to family's needs and schedules.

2. *Family-Based Ministry Model*: Programmatic structures remain unchanged, but each separate ministry plans and programs activities that intentionally draw generations together and invite parents to take part in the discipleship of their children and youth.

3. *Family-Equipping Model*: Although age-organized programs and events still exist, the ministry is completely restructured to draw generations together and invite parents to take part in the discipleship of their children and youth.

4. *Family-Integrated Model*: The church eliminates age-segregated programs and events. All or nearly all programs and events are multigenerational, with a strong focus on parents' responsibility to use their household as a context for evangelizing and discipling not only their own families but also others outside the faith community.[3]

It is obvious, then, that *Engaging Generation Z* argues for a reformation of youth ministry, not the abolition of it. It takes time, though, to implement major changes. As you can see, there is a wide spectrum of opinion on the "to do youth ministry or not to do youth ministry" continuum. One extreme is to perpetuate the status quo: offer increasingly bigger and better games and events, creep closer and closer to the world. Such an approach will not change things for the better.

On the other extreme, churches can totally eliminate youth ministry and be built on family units. Biblical ecclesiology, however, teaches neither extreme separation *nor* a church model built on family units. The church is the body of Christ, not a family conference.

Youth ministers, if we move to a model of helping parents be the main youth ministers to their children, if we emphasize far less segregation, games, and so on, you might think doing so will work you out of a job. Let me ask you, where has the way we have done youth ministry gotten us so far? What is the definition of insanity? Doing the same thing the same way every time and expecting different results. If your concern is maintaining a position or building your platform in youth ministry, please get out of the ministry now. It is not about us or our position or platform. It is about *Jesus* and leading youth and their family members to follow him as Savior and Lord.

---

3 Jones, *Family Ministry Guide*, 133.

I am not ready to say that youth ministry has no place. Youth ministry needs serious retooling, not abolishing—reforming, not razing. Youth ministry is needed because families are not raising the bar, parents often being the greatest hindrance to their children becoming radicals for Jesus. So just as youth need more training in evangelism, parents need help in raising a new generation. And youth pastors can play a vital role in both, especially when it comes to reaching and helping youth from non-Christian homes.[4]

Youth Ministry That Raises the Bar

What model should youth pastors use if they want to raise the bar? Well, I won't give you one model, but I will mention some healthy principles found in a number of models and reveal some practices for the type of youth ministry I've already described in previous chapters that involves parents, youth pastors, adult leaders, and students. I would warn you not to try to find a cookie-cutter model that you can place over your youth ministry and cut out what does not fit. Rather, take biblical principles from the following models and work with your leaders to develop one that fits your current ministry context.

You might have already figured out by what I have written in my chapters on orthodoxy, orthopathy, orthopraxy, and parents that I align pretty closely with the *family-equipping* model proposed by Timothy Paul Jones. Parents are the primary disciplers of students. We need to work as pastors, youth pastors, staff members, and ministry leaders to lead parents to Christ and disciple them. Youth pastors agree that parents are pivotal to the healthy spiritual development of students; however, most youth pastors rarely spend time with parents. In a recent study from *Lifeway Students*, Ben Trueblood reports:

> Seventy-two percent of student ministers say they spend an hour or less each week investing in the parents of those in

---

4   For another book related to this conversation regarding eliminating youth ministry, see Mark Senter, ed., *Four Views of Youth Ministry* (Grand Rapids: Zondervan, 2001).

their ministries (including 23 percent who don't spend any time with parents). Fifty-nine percent say they have not discipled or trained parents as a group. Sixty-seven percent of them say they invest in individual parents every few months or less (including 28 percent who rarely or never do).[5]

If we want to have parents who model biblical discipleship for their teenagers, we need to disciple them or provide those discipleship opportunities and relationships. By intentionally interacting with parents and insuring they are discipled, we will raise the bar in our youth ministries.

You have also seen me emphasize adult youth workers in this book. I have often referred to them as adult leaders. These folks work with the youth pastor in the church's youth ministry. They are also role models in discipleship that students can follow, particularly students who do not have parents who follow Christ. Youth pastors agree that it is imperative that they disciple their adult leaders and invest in them spiritually; however, very few youth pastors actually take time in their ministries to make discipling adult leaders a priority. Trueblood notes that 36 percent of leaders coach or train their adult volunteers every few months, while 35 percent of leaders coach or train them once a year or never. That's 71 percent of youth leaders who provide very little training for adult volunteers.[6]

Another area that needs attention in our youth ministries is the area of evangelism. Our churches are declining across denominational lines. Perhaps part of this decline in evangelism is reflected in a recent survey of youth pastors regarding their goals in youth ministry. According to the Barna Group, only 24 percent of youth pastors listed evangelism and outreach to teens as a goal of their youth ministry. The same study reveals that only 4 percent stated that evangelism of

---

5 Ben Trueblood, *Within Reach: The Power of Small Changes in Keeping Students Connected* (Nashville: Lifeway, 2018), 40.
6 Trueblood, *Within Reach*, 23.

parents of teens was a goal.[7] These statistics are especially staggering when one considers that contextualization of the gospel to win lost teens to Jesus is the reason for youth ministry in the first place. If we want to raise the bar in youth ministry, we need to repent of our lack of obedience to the Great Commission and renew a passion for making disciples of parents of teens and teens.

Addressing these areas will help us to create a strong model for youth ministry in our church context. There are also principles from existing models from which we can draw and apply to our ministries.

Doug Fields, student minister at the Saddleback Valley Community Church in California, is candid in his book *Purpose-Driven Youth Ministry* (*PDYM*). While it was written in the late '90s, this book is one that every youth pastor should read. Fields came to realize that building youth ministry on activities did not work: "I've been living with the weighty responsibility of developing a youth ministry that equips students, rather than a youth ministry that coordinates events. I don't want to direct programs; I want to disciple students."[8]

PDYM demonstrates how Fields moved to a purpose-driven model of ministry to students. Fields's book mirrors what his senior pastor, Rick Warren, said in *The Purpose-Driven Church*.[9] And that is as it should be. If you have a youth ministry whose purpose is distinct from that of the church, you are not a ministry of the church; you are a parachurch organization. The essential purpose of the church should not be changed for different groups within the church.

Nine components make up Fields's model:

1. *The power of God*—working through passionate leaders with pure hearts
2. *Purpose*—discovering why your ministry exists and following it up with communication and leadership

---

7   Barna Group, "Pastors and Parents Differ on Youth Ministry Goals," 2017, https://www.barna.com/research/pastors-parents-differ-youth-minis-try-goals.

8   Fields, *Purpose-Driven Youth Ministry*, 18.

9   Rick Warren, *The Purpose Driven Church* (Grand Rapids: Zondervan, 1995).

3. *Potential audience*—identifying which students are the target for the purposes
4. *Programs*—deciding what programs will reach your potential audience and help fulfill God's purposes
5. *Process*—displaying your programs so you can help students move toward spiritual maturity
6. *Planned values*—defining what values will strengthen your ministry and enhance your purposes
7. *Parents*—teaming up with the family for a stronger youth ministry and church
8. *Participating leaders*—finding volunteers and developing them into ministers who fulfill the purposes
9. *Perseverance*—learning how to survive the overwhelming responsibilities, discipline problems, and the adventure of change[10]

Fields begins by noting his own pilgrimage from the typical youth minister who frantically tries to please people, provide programs, and create the "hype." His honest confession—how he learned that his walk with God was paramount—demonstrates the need of the hour in youth ministry. What did he learn? "No youth ministry idea or program can compete with God's power working in and through you as he gives you a passion for students and you give him a pure heart."[11] Enough of youth ministry focuses on programs and techniques; we need passion and truth. Fields's book will help you build a solid ministry to youth and raise the bar in the areas I've noted above and throughout this book.

A similar passion is seen in *The Seven Checkpoints* by Stanley and Hall, where content, they argue, should drive context:

It is one thing to put together a summer camp. It is quite another thing to create the optimal five-day environment for

10   Fields, *Purpose-Driven Youth Ministry*, 19–22.
11   Fields, *Purpose-Driven Youth Ministry*, 39.

teenagers to rethink their whole approach to friendship. . . .
When content is the focus, the context becomes vitally
important. This approach to youth ministry will motivate
you and your leadership to raise the bar programmatically.[12]

Stanley and Hall offer the following seven checkpoints to build
a youth ministry:

1. *Authentic faith*—God can be trusted
2. *Spiritual disciplines*—devotional life
3. *Moral boundaries*—personal purity
4. *Healthy friendships*—choosing friends
5. *Wise choices*—decision-making
6. *Ultimate authority*—submission to God's authority
7. *Others first*—humility and service[13]

Stanley and Hall's model, as well as Fields's, addresses the important issues of the Christian life. But churches can raise the bar yet higher
in the vital areas of theological truth and biblical knowledge, and the
practical area of personal evangelism. Remember my conversation
of parents, youth pastors, and youth leaders discipling students to
develop orthodoxy, orthopathy, and orthopraxy. The content in this
second half of *Engaging Generation Z* is key to you raising the bar in
your student ministry.

So, youth pastor, it's up to you. Will you apply the principles from
these models and raise the bar in your youth ministry?

---

12 Stanley and Hall, *Seven Checkpoints*, 8–9.
13 Stanley and Hall, *Seven Checkpoints*, 8–9.

13

RITES OF PASSAGE
SEASONS OF CHANGE

For I know the plans I have for you, declares the
LORD, plans for welfare and not for evil, to give
you a future and a hope.

—Jeremiah 29:11

They had been waiting since they were thirteen for this
moment. Twin eighteen-year-old sons knelt before their
father, who was dressed in a ceremonial kilt bearing the
family tartan and sporting a Prince Charlie jacket and bowtie.
He held a Scottish claymore with both hands on the hilt pointed
to the ground. Noah and Micah repeated this oath after their
father:

Be loyal of hands and mouth and serve every man as
best you may. Seek the fellowship of good men; hearken
to their words and remember them. Be humble and
courteous wherever thou go, boasting not nor talking
overmuch, neither be dumb altogether. Look to it that
no lady or damsel be in reproach through your default,
nor any woman of whatsoever quality. And if you fall
into company where men speak with disrespect of any
woman, show by gracious words that it pleaseth you
not, and depart. The office of knight is to promote faith
in Jesus Christ as Lord of Lords, King of Kings and the
only Savior and to protect those who seek to worship

in his name anywhere upon the face of this earth that
he has made.[1]

I then lifted the claymore and tapped them twice on one shoulder
and once on the other. I told them to rise as knights.

This knighting ceremony for my twin sons was one of the proudest
moments I've had as a father. My family comes from knights who hailed
from the border of Scotland and England. Our family crest includes a
castle tower with the words "I hope in God" over it. After I knighted
the boys, I placed silver rings with the family crest on their fingers. I
wear an identical ring every day. Then, their grandfathers spoke about
how they see Christ in their lives. Then one by one, friends and family
members took time to pay them tribute. At the end of the ceremony,
my pastor came to me and said, "Tim, that's one of the most beautiful
ceremonies I've ever seen. I've never seen anything like it."

His words made me feel affirmed and grieved at the same time. I
grieved because I knew that many teenagers would never experience an
important rite of passage like the ones my children have experienced.
I had never thought about such ceremonies as a father until I read
a book by Richard Lewis titled *Raising a Modern-Day Knight*. Lewis
says fathers are failing their sons at three points:

1. *Defining manhood:* "Telling a boy to 'be a man' without defining manhood is like saying, 'be a success.' It sounds good.
   But, practically, it takes you nowhere."
2. *Directional process:* "What [a son] needs is a specific language
   and training that takes him to the place where, like the apostle Paul, he can say, 'When I became a man, I did away with
   childish things.'"
3. *Ceremony:* "How many dads today think of formally commem-
   orating their sons' progress or passage to manhood? Very few."[2]

---

1   "The Oath of a Knight," http://www.knightforhire.com/oathandscoutinfo.html.
2   Robert Lewis, *Raising a Modern-Day Knight* (Wheaton, IL: Tyndale House,
    1997), 10.

Lewis notes the case of Jeffrey Dahmer. Dahmer, who performed the gruesome killings of seventeen people, was convicted in 1992 and was killed by an inmate two years later. He was raised by his mother and father. Dahmer's story is not, then, the tale of a broken home. It's the story of a dad who was around geographically, but not *there* emotionally. Likewise, Dylan Klebold and Eric Harris—the gunmen at Columbine—lived with their parents. So troubled youth cannot be blamed simply on broken homes. While the breakdown of the family is a huge factor in youth problems, other causes are far more complex.

Theories of child raising abound, each trailed by controversy over its validity. But there's one fact that all parents agree upon. Life changes when you have kids. Theories about child-rearing move instantly from the hypothetical to the real. It is one thing to give advice to others based on your theory of this or that; it is altogether another thing to apply those theories to your children.

So when my sons approached the youth years, I was struck with the fact that, as a youth pastor, I could minister to teens and send them away with their parents. Now I had teens I could not send away because they were mine. Suddenly, all of those bad things I had thought about the parents of my students came back to haunt me. Maybe those folks were just as clueless about what to do as I was right then.

Lewis's book was a great help to me. But my primary source for guidance was Scripture. Following conversion, baptism serves as a significant ceremony, publicly demonstrating the believer's identification with Christ. Marriage is another beautiful ceremony that marks both an achievement and a life-changing event. In my church, we observe the dedication of a child, which actually is the dedication of the *parents,* celebrated in a meaningful ceremony. But what then for that child?

We have replaced ceremonies with banquets, and we have trivialized important steps in the lives of young adults. Now we no longer teach or recognize such steps. It is time for a rebirth of rites of passage. But these will be significant only if they serve to mark genuine turning points in the lives of those participating in such ceremonies.

Our culture does have rites of passage: moving from middle school to high school, obtaining a driver's license, graduating from high school. These are still officially recognized but are the property of culture, not the church.

So when my sons turned thirteen, I had a ceremony similar to the one described at the beginning of this chapter; however, in this ceremony, I dubbed them pages. I invited significant men in their lives to speak into them. They encouraged them to pursue godliness and live honorably. I spoke to them about honoring their mom and sisters. I explained that pages in the time of the knights were beginners at learning the code of chivalry. I read the same oath that they took when they became knights. It speaks of how to treat women. As they were just starting to take karate, their sensei and I both talked about self-discipline and the importance of defending people who are vulnerable and need help. I also took this opportunity to talk about the spiritual battle against sin and the importance of a daily time of prayer and Bible reading in their lives.

I noticed a change in my sons after the ceremony. They treated their mom and sisters with a new respect. They sought to protect them when they were out and about. They began to understand the need to take responsibility for their actions.

Although I'm not convinced that the evangelical church will come to a consensus on what rites of passage to observe or how, I pray that we'll all come to a conviction about the importance of raising up a generation of godly young men and women. To that end, here are some possible transitions/rites.

Age twelve. David Black refers to this as the age-twelve transition, one of the most vital turning points of life. At age twelve, Jesus was in the temple, teaching about his heavenly Father. He and other Jewish youth went through a Bar Mitzvah ceremony. Even to the present day, this ceremony is seen as "a period when young people are obligated to control their own desires, accept responsibility for mature religious actions, and assume adult community responsibilities."[3] In the twentieth century, the Bat Mitzvah was developed for young women.

---

3 David Alan Black, *The Myth of Adolescence* (Yorba Linda, CA: Davidson, 1998), 60.

For centuries, cultures around the world have recognized a time of turning toward adulthood at about this age:

- Sitting Bull, the mighty chief, spent days alone in the wilderness at this age;
- Masai tribesmen have a similar ceremony, as do young men in Nigeria and other African cultures; and
- Amish boys in some areas are taught to run the entire farm at around age twelve.

Black offers excellent advice on and examples of how to hold a ceremony. This includes both a public ceremony and a private letter from a parent to a child.

Increasing numbers of evangelical parents are taking their children through a service similar to this when their child turns twelve. Imagine the youth pastor or another significant adult in your church taking the parents and the student to a meal, where he explains the purpose of the vital years to come and the church's role—to help their child to adulthood. This would be not only a good starting point for raising the bar, but it could be a means of witness to unchurched parents. Parents actively involved in your church could be shown how to observe a Christian rite of passage or similar ceremony.

While the twelve-year-old rite is the major turning point, other ceremonies like the following could help to guide a youth into adulthood.

Age sixteen. Paralleling the major step of responsibility of a driver's license, a ceremony or perhaps a banquet when a youth turns sixteen is an excellent way to convey to a person what it means to be a man or woman of God. A group of men, highly respected as Christians, taking time individually to explain to a young man turning sixteen what it means to be a godly man could have a lifelong impact. The same could be said for a young woman. We had a special party for my daughter Karissa when she turned sixteen. It included key people in her life writing cards to her of encouragement to be the woman of God she's called to be. After she turned sixteen, my wife Angela took her on an overnight trip during which they went through a special curriculum called *Passport 2 Identity*. (This program is a follow up to the excellent program called *Passport 2 Purity*, which we took each of our children through at the age of 10.) *Passport 2 Identity* focuses on authentic womanhood (or manhood), owning your faith, building godly relationships and living out your faith on mission. Journeying through this curriculum during the two-day trip was another encouraging rite of passage for Karissa, during which she was reminded to find her identity in Christ.[4]

Age sixteen is already a critical transition in American culture. A young person getting a driver's license has huge implications for youth ministry. So many youth become less involved in church when they get a car and have more control over their time. Lower involvement can be laid partly on parents, as an alarming number of church youth are not only allowed but encouraged to work on Sundays. And we wonder why they drop out of church when they are on their own. They learn it from their churchgoing parents!

Youth ministries can provide valuable assistance to families by helping parents prepare children for the vital step of responsibility of driving. Rather than bemoaning the decline of church attendance by older youth who drive, churches can provide more challenging ministries using the growing maturity and responsibility of students. As young people move from the "do it because I tell you" relationship with their parents to an increasing ability and need to make responsible decisions, churches can help students step up spiritually even as they grow up socially. Churches can grant students opportunities to exercise their spiritual gifts, leading in worship and other ministries in the church. They also can lead younger students in small group Bible study.

Age eighteen or high school graduation. While your children are still young, set a standard for them to give a summer, semester, or year following high school to the mission field. Begin challenging youth

---

4   Family Life, *Passport2Purity* (Little Rock, AR: FamilyLife, 2012); Family Life, *Passport2Identity* (Little Rock, AR: FamilyLife, 2016).

to prepare for spending the first year of their lives after high school in missions somewhere around the world. What a way to unleash an army to the world!

Marriage. Nothing other than conversion matters more than marriage. This is the only rite of passage today still deemed worthy by most to be consistently recognized as a ceremony. But if earlier rites were observed, might not adults be more prepared for this vital covenant?

Along the way, give youth increasing types of chores and responsibilities around the house. Teach them to be responsible with their finances. (Tithing started early makes a difference!) Let them lead in church to the level they can. This could be an area your church needs to examine.

A Word to Fathers

I frequently have adults and young people approach me to compliment my sons and what gentlemen they are. My wife Angela and I also hear frequently positive comments about our daughters. People compliment them about how they carry themselves as young women. Our sons and daughters did not develop the values they have regarding what it means to be a young woman or young man by osmosis. They were taught these values by my wife and me.

Young men learn to be rude. They learn to be gross. They learn to speak coarsely to women. And cultural emphasis on neutralizing genders over the past few years has caused too many dads to fail when it comes to teaching their sons how to treat the opposite sex with honor and respect. It seems that the radical feminist movement in America has not only robbed women of their femininity; it has robbed men of their masculinity. But I refuse to bow to the policies of the politically correct. It is a sad day when the word *gentlemen* is only seen on bathroom doors or on signs advertising adult strip clubs. It is also a sad day when women are objectified by our society. Young women need to learn their intrinsic value and beauty; they are made in the image of God and are "fearfully and wonderfully made" (Gen. 1:26–27; Ps. 139:14).

As illustrated at the beginning of this chapter, dads teaching their sons how to be men has lost priority. Dads today were not taught it themselves, so they don't know where to start. (And are moms teaching their daughters what it means to be not only a woman, but a *lady*? Is not the problem of teenaged ladies dressing immodestly an issue their mothers should address?)

How is a dad to teach a son to be a man? Lewis gives helpful counsel:

1. *A real man rejects passivity.* I spoke to a men's retreat in Denver, Colorado. In a demonstration of brokenness, a leader in the church confessed, "My son has been a problem lately, becoming more rebellious. How have I dealt with this? I simply started working longer hours." This man's candid confession demonstrates our culture's view of Dad as a provider above all else. But this dad realized he was simply being passive, hiding at work, hoping the problem would go away.

2. *A real man accepts responsibility.* Dads, you are responsible for your children's spiritual nurture. Yet so many dads relinquish this to moms or to the church. It is biblically inconsistent and personally irresponsible for a father to be known as a reliable worker at the office, a dependable volunteer at church, yet be uninvolved in the spiritual, emotional, and relational upbringing of his children.

3. *A real man leads courageously.* The quota for Christian wimps has been met. Dads, good for you if you provide for your family, but even lost dads do that. Do your children see you stand courageously for Jesus?

4. *A real man expects the greater reward.* I have an incredible job. I teach the greatest students on earth, get to preach in some of the finest churches in America, and have written many books. But all that pales in comparison to my family. I have turned down some incredible opportunities—leading a major prayer summit by Promise Keepers; speaking to the largest crowd in my life in Asia. Other opportunities have come and gone.

Yet I refused to accept them. Why? Because I already made a commitment to my family. I believe God rewards faithfulness more than opportunism. Don't misunderstand; at times I've missed family events or a ball game for the Lord. I don't believe the family should be an idol. But after God himself, my family is my second priority. My ministry comes third.[5]

Men, your children need you to be godly.

Richard Baxter, the great Puritan pastor of centuries past, said the only way we will see true reformation is to see it first in the home. Increasingly, parents are discovering the truth of Baxter's remark. We need to look to Scripture and share the biblical way to family life in the face of feminism and other assaults on the home.

No parent is perfect. It is important to let our kids know that we are fallen creatures seeking to pursue Christ and his will in our lives just like we hope they are. In our imperfections, it's important that our children know that we love the Lord Jesus Christ, and we love them. They need to hear their parents say, "I love you," on a regular basis and show the truth of these words in their actions and their words.

I started this chapter by describing a rite of passage ceremony involving my sons, Noah and Micah. Hear the words that they wrote to me. They prove that what I'm writing is more than theory.

I Pray I Grow into a Man Like You

Happy Birthday, to a man I aspire to be like. Dad, I don't really know how to start, you give and sacrifice so much for your family!

In a world where having a dad is rare and having a genuine and loving one is almost unheard of, you stand out among many imitators! I am constantly surrounded by friends and loved ones who's fathers have either been absent or abusive, and you have been nothing but kind. I mean that with no disrespect to them; however, I am

---

5 Lewis, *Raising a Modern-Day Knight*, 51–59.

grateful, to say the least, for you sticking around and giving a care about us.

When Micah and I were still not even a year old, you sacrificed the first year with us in order to help secure a future for us by serving overseas on your deployment, thank you! You don't talk much about it, you don't brag about it, but you are a peaceful warrior and have a true heart that reflects that of Christ.

I could say a lot of things and still not communicate even a third of my love for you, but I will say that you are my superhero still. You are my Liam Neeson in *Taken,* my Bruce Willis in *Unbroken* and my Tom Cruise in *The Last Samurai,* to name a few fictional characters who don't measure up to you; yet, I see pieces of you in them. Thank you for always pushing me to do my best, thank you for never giving up on me, and thank you for always pointing to Christ in your victories! I love that I get to see you on campus and that we can talk even for brief moments in the day, having a professor for a dad is pretty cool!

—Noah

Dad,
I pray I grow into a man like you.

—Micah

All the accolades I could receive as a pastor, professor, and author will always take a back seat to words like this spoken from my children. They are the flock with which God has blessed me. I love all four of them. I love my wife Angela even more. And I love God more than her. My family would not want it any other way.

So What?

You might read this chapter and wonder, *How does this relate to engaging Generation Z?* Well, this generation faces a great deal of confusion regarding gender identity and gender roles in our culture.

It needs moms and dads who are willing to step up to the plate and disciple their students regarding what it looks like to be a godly man or a godly woman. Walking their teens through these rites of passage are a great way for parents to help them develop a biblical grounding regarding gender, gender identity, and roles. Such intentional discipleship by parents also helps students who follow Christ to communicate to their peers what the Bible teaches regarding these issues. Perhaps, armed with such truth, believers in Generation Z can point their friends toward Scripture with the goal of growing mighty men and women of God.

CONCLUSION

RAISE THE BAR

> Command and teach these things. Let no one despise you for your youth, but set the believers an example in speech, in conduct, in love, in faith, in purity.
>
> —1 Timothy 4:11–12

To sum up, this is what youth ministers must do:

1. Stop treating youth like children who are finishing childhood, and start treating them like young adults moving into adulthood. The myth of adolescence is just that—a myth.
2. Reduce the age segregation of youth from the life of the church by engaging parents in your youth ministry.
3. Raise the bar in what we teach in terms of both biblical orthodoxy, orthopathy, and orthopraxy. *Belief and affections,* not only behavior, must be changed. We must also help our students worship with their minds, souls, and strength.
4. Disciple and equip parents who disciple their teenagers. Emphasize their role as the primary disciplers of their students.
5. Disciple and equip adult leaders who share the gospel and serve as role models that students can follow in orthodoxy, orthopathy, and orthopraxy.
6. Work with the pastor, staff, and church leaders to disciple children, youth, and parents.
7. Help parents develop rites of passage that will help them develop young men and women who are examples to adults and their peers as children grow up.

I was deployed on Operation Noble Eagle in September of 2001. Eventually my orders switched to Operation Enduring Freedom, which would keep me deployed from September 2001 to August of 2002. At the time I received my orders to deploy, I was serving as a youth pastor in a church about twenty-eight miles south of Louisville where I attended seminary. I had served as the church's youth pastor since January of 1996. Students who were sixth graders when I first started as youth pastor were looking forward to their graduation in May of 2002. I too was looking forward to watching them graduate.

From the time I began as their youth pastor, I discipled them to be leaders in their schools and in the church. I believed that they would reach any bar I set for them. If I set the bar low, they'd reach it. If I set it high, they'd reach it. I decided to set the bar high.

I taught them doctrine, including some of the things I was learning about biblical and systematic theology in my classes at the seminary. We read through books on the spiritual disciplines. They took part in ministry and missions, helping people in the community and serving communities in other states. They helped to lead in our midweek Bible studies for the youth group and in our worship services. Some of them sang in the choir or helped to take up the offering in the worship service. They served on our student leadership team, helping to plan the entire calendar year for our youth ministry. We did not just plan events, but gave biblical purposes for having each event and an understanding of how they fit into the broader mission and strategy of the youth group. By the time I deployed, these seniors had gone through six years of me, adult leaders, and parents pouring into them spiritually.

When I deployed, they didn't skip a beat. The youth group grew while I was gone. The students stepped up and led the music and worship for the youth group. They grew in their Bible studies and led devotionals for each other. They also had an interim youth pastor who discipled them until I got back from the deployment.

I'm so proud of that youth group and how God used them. Particularly, I'm proud of the seniors who spent five years leading beside me and their sixth year in youth group stepping up and leading without me. That youth group continues to affirm my belief that when we raise the bar in youth ministry, students will reach it every time.